GROUP RELATIONS
CONFERENCES

Reviewing and Exploring Theory, Design,
Role-Taking and Application

GROUP RELATIONS CONFERENCES

Reviewing and Exploring Theory, Design,
Role-Taking and Application

*Louisa Diana Brunner, Avi Nutkevitch,
& Mannie Sher*

KARNAC

First published in 2006 by
Karnac Books
118 Finchley Road, London NW3 5HT

British Library Cataloguing in Publication Data

A C.I.P. for this book is available from the British Library

ISBN13: 978 1 85575 475 1
ISBN10: 1 85575 475 4

Edited, designed, and typeset by RefineCatch Ltd, Bungay, Suffolk
Printed in Great Britain

www.karnacbooks.com

CONTENTS

ACKNOWLEDGEMENTS

We thank OFEK and the Tavistock Institute for their support for a new and untried venture to extend our understanding of Group Relations conferences and their application to the study of society and organisations. In doing so, we also acknowledge the profound contribution of Eric Miller to our knowledge and experience of Group Relations, to the development of both institutions and to the international Group Relations network. We are grateful to the authors and contributors to this book and to the participants of the first Belgirate Conference who shared in the task of adding to Group Relations conference understandings. The editors also want to remember Faith Gabelnick who contributed so much to the development of Group Relations in the USA, who passed away a few months after her attendance at the Belgirate Conference.

ABOUT THE EDITORS AND CONTRIBUTORS

Editors

Louisa Diana Brunner, MSc, is a management and organisational consultant. She carries out selection and career counseling for the MBA Courses at the Bocconi School of Management, Milan. Her main areas of intervention and interest are leadership, organisational culture, Group Relations, team-building, family business, generational transitions and executive coaching. She teaches on the course on organisational development, promoted by CESMA (Milan), Il NodoGroup (Turin) and Tavistock Consultancy Service (London). Member of OFEK.

Avi Nutkevitch, PhD, is a clinical psychologist, psychoanalyst and organisational consultant. He is a full member of the Israel Psychoanalytic Society and teaches at the Israel Psychoanalytic Institute and other postgraduate programs for psychotherapy. He is a founding member and former Chair of OFEK, the Israel Association for the Study of Group and Organisational Processes. He is currently Co-Director and Faculty of the Program in Organisational Consultation and Development: a Psychoanalytic-Systemic Approach. He holds a senior teaching position on the MBA programme of the College of Management in Rishon Le'Tzion.

Mannie Sher, BA, TQAP, FBAP, is a Principal Social Scientist and Director of the Group Relations Programme at the Tavistock Institute, London. He manages organisational development and change projects and consults to top management of organisations on the role of leadership in effecting strategic change. He is a Fellow of the British Association of Psychotherapists (BAP) and a practising psychoanalytical psychotherapist. Mannie has published on subjects of consultancy, leadership, organisational development, ethics and corruption. He is a member of ISPSO, OFEK and OPUS.

Contributors

Jan Baker, MA, works as an organisational consultant and psychotherapist. She directs two annual Group Relations conferences for Birkbeck College, University of London. Jan also works as a Tutor on the Master's programmes in psychodynamic counselling at Birkbeck College and regularly consults to organisations in the arena of health and education. Her background is in teaching, youth work and training and she is particularly interested in the application of Group Relations work.

Siv Boalt Boëthius, PhD, is a professor at Stockholm University, psychoanalyst and Board member of the Swedish Group Relations Organisation (AGSLO). She was formerly head of a University College in Stockholm and visiting professor at Copenhagen University. She works mainly in consultation and research. Her main areas of research are group and organisational psychology and she has published widely on these subjects.

Gabi Bonwitt, MA, is a clinical psychologist and a member of the International Psychoanalytic Association. He works in the Israel public health service and in private practice as a psychoanalyst and organisational consultant. He teaches at the Haifa and Bar Ilan universities and on the psychotherapy course of the Israel Psychoanalytic Institute. Gabi is currently a Board member of OFEK, the Israel Society for the Study of Group and Organisational Processes, and is a Director of its Group Relations conferences. He directed the first two Israeli conferences on *Sexual Violence in the Family and Society*. He also has an interest in the production of film documentaries on social matters.

Mira Erlich-Ginor, MA, is a clinical psychologist and psychoanalyst. She is a training analyst and Chair of the Education Committee of the Israel Psychoanalytic Society. She is also an organisational consultant and a member of the Board and Faculty of the Program in Organisational Consultation and Development: A Psychoanalytic-Systemic Approach, run by OFEK and the Sigmund Freud Centre at the Hebrew University in Jerusalem. Mira is a Founding Member and Past Chair of OFEK and she has been a staff member and Director of many Group Relations conferences in Israel and abroad. She was among the initiators and staff of the German and Israeli conferences: *The Past in the Present*.

Lilian A. J. Hupkens, MSC MPC, studied physics and industrial engineering and worked both as a management consultant and executive director. Being interested in organisational dynamics, she studied psychoanalytical counselling, acquiring a Masters degree and further trained as a group therapist. Her main interest lies in integrating both approaches – psychoanalytic theory and insights with broader traditional organisational sciences. Her activities are training professionals, coaching executives, research and writing.

Karen Izod, MA, CQSW, is an independent organisational change consultant (KIzod Consulting) specialising in helping individuals and organisations create structures and positions to work to best effect. She is a Principal Associate at the Tavistock Institute, where she co-leads the Executive Coaching and Development Programme, and is Faculty for the MA and Qualification in Advanced Organisational Consultation. She is a member of the Tavistock Institute's Group Relations Committee.

Olya Khaleelee, MA, is a corporate psychologist, organisational consultant and psychoanalytic psychotherapist. She has worked with the Tavistock Institute for over 20 years in developing Group Relations both in the UK and abroad, has been on the staff of many conferences and was the first female director of the Leicester Conference. She is currently director of the Institute's conference: 'Leaders in Changing Organisations'.

Ross A. Lazar, BA(Hons), MA, is an Art Historian and a teacher with a special interest in early and special education. He taught History of Art at Leeds University and Leeds Polytechnic and later taught at the Weavers' Fields Special School for the Emotionally Disturbed in London's East End. He is a child and adolescent psychotherapist (Tavistock Clinic) and worked as a psychotherapist and family therapist in the Child Guidance Clinic, London Borough of Newham, the Marlborough Day Hospital and the Child and Adolescent Psychotherapy Clinic of the Munich Technical University. Currently he is in private practice and also works extensively as a supervisor and organisational consultant throughout Europe.

Ilana Litvin, MA, MSc, is a clinical psychologist and a psychoanalytically-oriented psychotherapist, organisational consultant and executive coach in private practice. She is trained and active in the area of Group Relations, currently particularly interested in applying and adapting Group Relations concepts, technique and culture to social issues. She is the Chairperson of OFEK.

Carl Mack, Jr, PhD, is Senior Lecturer at the California School of Business and Organisational Studies and at the Alliant International University, Fresno/Sacramento, California. He is President of the Board of Directors of Youth In Focus, Oakland, California and Principal Consultant, Abuya Works, Davis, California. Until his recent retirement, he was Superintendent of the Del Paso Heights School District, Sacramento, California.

Anton Obholzer, BSc, MB, ChB, DPM, FRCPsych, formerly Director of the Tavistock Centre, is a psychoanalyst, organisational consultant and coach with a particular interest in strategic leadership and the management of change. He pursues these activities through consulting to organisations, teams and individuals; through the coaching of senior members of staff; and by lecturing and teaching in a variety of settings in the UK and abroad. His has visiting professorships at the universities of Vienna, Graz and Innsbruck and he is a senior fellow at the Strategic Leadership Centre, Insead International Business School, Paris.

Allan Shafer MA, D. Litt et Phil., is a clinical psychologist and socioanalyst working privately as a psychotherapist and organisation consultant in Perth, Western Australia. He was Director of Group

Relations Programmes for the former Australian Institute of Socio-Analysis. He has directed or been a staff member of Group Relations conferences in Australia, the UK and Israel. He is a founding member of Group Relations Australia.

Joseph Triest, PhD, is a clinical psychologist, Training Analyst of the Israel Psychoanalytic Institute and organisational consultant. He is the owner of the Triest-Sarig private clinic, a lecturer at Tel-Aviv University's general BA programme and the Group Facilitators Programme. He supervises and teaches at the Israel Psychoanalytical Institute and on the 'Geha' psychotherapy course. He is a Member of OFEK, the Israel Association for the Study of Group and Organisational Processes and is a Co-director and Faculty in the Program in Organisational Consultation and Development: a Psychoanalytic-Systemic Approach.

FOREWORD

I am honoured to have been asked to write a foreword for this book that arises from the Belgirate Conference. In considering whether or not I was willing and able to do so, I found myself obliged to address the fundamental question of whether some of the criticisms of the Group Relations movement I (and others) had held over recent years were justified or not. These criticisms essentially fell into two categories: firstly that the Group Relations conference model was nowadays of lesser relevance in the business world because it required a time commitment which was no longer compatible with the pace of commercial life; secondly that the Group Relations world had some of the characteristics of a global, somewhat incestuous sect. This is a fate that not uncommonly befalls many a new idea and its adherents. These two categories of criticism are related in that they both contributed to such conferences increasingly drawing mainly from the body of those already committed and thus failing to communicate with those working at the coalface.

It was encouraging to find that these very issues were addressed in some of the key contributions in this volume. On reflection I came to the conclusion that although there was some truth in the criticisms voiced above they were of no greater magnitude than was to be expected from any new idea or technique that has to find its place in the world community of ideas. It is integral to such a process, and inevitable, that new ideas will meet resistance and envious attack.

Importantly, there is now new and impressive evidence, partly represented by the papers in this book, that the 'Tavistock' Group Relations model is in a new and vital phase of development: It has moved on from a phase of preoccupation with conference design, with particular reference to the relation between stability and innovation, to a phase of application in all sorts of different contexts including the commercial world.

Group Relations ideas have always had a degree of application in the public sector; particularly in health, social services and education. This is also true of the voluntary sector. What is relatively new is that there is now substantial evidence that 'Tavistock/Leicester' Group Relations ideas are being taught and applied increasingly in business schools and in the business field. It is true that the 'parentage' of these ideas is often not acknowledged and that the ideas sail under a variety of flags: e.g. 'emotional intelligence'; 360-degree feedback and so on. What they all have in common though is the idea that there are unconscious or pre-conscious processes at work; that these concealed processes involve group and inter-group phenomena and that they can be worked on and understood. It is increasingly realised that competent authority, leadership and followership depend on an awareness of these phenomena.

These factors, and others such as the need to be aware of the dynamics associated with groups of various sizes; of work versus basic assumption groups; of the need to be aware of the primary task, are the cornerstones that inform the concepts of the Group-Relations model. The fact these concepts are often nowadays dressed up as mentoring, coaching or consultancy, doesn't matter. What does matter is that these techniques are heavily dependent on the conceptual and training frameworks that have been developed over the past fifty years or so in the Tavistock Groups Relations model. In doing so the wheel has come full circle and what we have that is new is a Renaissance of Group Relations ideas. This book gives further impetus to the pace of this productive wheel of change.

Anton Obholzer
Psychoanalyst and Organisational Consultant
Formerly Director of the Tavistock Centre
February 2006

PREFACE

An international community of Group Relations practitioners met at Belgirate on the shores of Lake Maggiore, Italy, in November 2003 to reflect on and debate contemporary issues in Group Relations and their application to the changing needs of organisations and society. The conference aimed to study Tavistock Group Relations conferences via an innovative integration of experiential, reflective and didactic elements. There were two keynote lectures and eight parallel lectures and other group events that focused on the theory, design, role taking and application of Group Relations conferences.

The conference was sponsored by OFEK – the Israel Association for the Study of Group and Organisational Processes and the Tavistock Institute, London. Membership of the conference was international, 52 delegates drawn from 11 countries. Eligibility to conference membership was by having had previous staff roles in Tavistock-Leicester type Group Relations conferences. The background to this conference, the reason for choosing Italy as a venue and the role played by the two co-sponsoring organisations are described in Chapter 1.

This book reflects the unique culture of the Belgirate Conference, namely combining traditional and experiential modes of developing new ideas and knowledge; and in order to further the field of Group Relations. The conference was conceived as a space, or a 'container', for generating ideas through a collective effort and exploration, in a continuous interplay between theory and experience during the conference itself and during the pre- and post-conference phases. Thus, the Belgirate Conference encouraged people to present their ideas on the conference's topic and articulate and conceptualise them through writing elements of the 'here and now' dynamics of the conference.

Thus, this book contains the collection of papers presented at the conference plus two additional papers. They represent a collective picture of the value of Group Relations thinking in addressing organisational and societal needs.

The structure of the book is built around the following themes:

- *Structure, design and learning in Group Relations conferences.* These themes are addressed in the keynote lectures by Olya Khaleelee and Mira Erlich-Ginor, who through presenting a conceptual frame and sharing their personal experiences as consultants and directors, also challenge and question traditional approaches to Group Relations conferences.
- *Themed conferences and Group Relations conference methodology.* The papers by Ilana Litvin and Gabi Bonwitt and by Ross Lazar tackle difficult social issues on sexual abuse in families and Israeli society and the tribulations of two German psycho-analytic institutions. Their papers demonstrate the usefulness of Group Relations conference methodology in addressing complex conflicts and trauma.
- *The application of Group Relations conferences methodology to pro-fessional roles.* Papers by Siv Boalt Boëthius, Karen Izod and Carl Mack deal with working with multiple roles in a university in Europe, career development and ownership in a global phar-maceutical company and the application of the methodology to the public school system in the USA respectively.
- *Researching Group Relations conference methodology and outcome.* Papers by Lilian Hupkins and Allan Shafer help us to hold on to the 'scientific' underpinning of Group Relations conferences through their investigations of the nature of applied learning in terms of motivation and outcome of attendance at

Group Relations conferences in different countries and in different settings.

- *Post Conference reflections: group processes and leadership.* Jan Baker in her paper reflects on the emergence of spontaneous small groups in Group Relations conferences and their meaning for the 'system'. Josef Triest's paper re-evaluates the Group Relations model in the light of notions of 'twinship' – two co-sponsoring organisations, two male conference managers, two female keynote speakers, etc.

This book will interest members of the Group Relations community and others who are familiar with and utilise Tavistock Group Relations thinking in their research, consultancy, management or teaching roles. This book will be useful too for people who are not familiar with the Tavistock Group Relations approach, but who may wish to dip into it in order to find out more and learn about an approach to understanding groups, organisations and society that is both theoretical and intensely practical. The structure of the book is designed to convey to the reader a set of values inherent in Group Relations work and the passion and commitment of the people doing it. The book may serve as an inspiration to people who believe that issues that influence our lives at work and in society are complex and need more sophisticated tools to deepen understanding and lead to change.

This book appears during the celebrations of the Tavistock Institute's 60th and OFEK's 20th anniversaries, and is testimony to the intellectual vigour of the Tavistock Institute which continues to refresh and develop its intellectual traditions. It is also evident of OFEK's coming of age as an organisation and its expansion from a primary focus on experiential learning to intellectual and theoretical contributions to the field of Group Relations.

Louisa Diana Brunner, Avi Nutkevitch, & Mannie Sher
February, 2006

GROUP RELATIONS CONFERENCES
Reviewing and Exploring Theory, Design,
Role-Taking and Application

Introduction

Group Relations Conferences

Reviewing and exploring theory, design, role-taking and application*

Avi Nutkevitch and Mannie Sher

I n November 2003, a four-day residential conference on Group Relations conferences for previous Group Relations conference staff members was held in Belgirate, Italy, organised by Avi Nutkevitch of OFEK, a Group Relations organisation in Israel and Mannie Sher of The Tavistock Institute, London.

Background

The primary task of the conference was to review and explore the theory and design, the taking up of roles in, and the application of Group Relations conferences. The Belgirate Conference, as it came to be known, was intended to be a 'space' of the kind that is not normally available during Group Relations conferences themselves. It was intended to review and explore dilemmas and questions that lie

* This paper was published in the journal *Organisational and Social Dynamics*, Vol. 4. No. 1. 2004 and summarises the main features of creating and producing the first Belgirate Conference.

at the heart of Group Relations work. The absence of appropriate opportunities to explore these questions is a source of frustration and guilt. It is an abiding principle in Group Relations conferences that staff works through their own particular conceptual and other issues, just as conference members are expected to do. This principle is related to and is in the service of the undertaking by staff to do everything possible that promotes the conference's primary task and of furthering the learning of the dynamic relatedness between individuals, groups, organisations and society. The Belgirate Conference was, therefore, designed as a particular structured opportunity for reviewing, exploring and learning more about the different aspects of Group Relations conference design, dynamic and delivery. The conference was conceptualised and designed as a 'transitional space' that would contain traditional scientific modes of learning, such as lectures and discussions, and an experiential 'here and now' mode of learning.

This blend of modes had its difficulties and complexities, but it also provided potential for creative learning and exploration. OFEK and The Tavistock Institute joined together to produce and sponsor the Belgirate Conference. The two organisations and their leaders had enjoyed long-term close working relationships in developing Group Relations in their respective countries. Their working relationship and their close personal relationship, as well as the physical facilities that their organisations were able to provide, facilitated the creation of the Belgirate Conference. The conference had been planned to take place in Israel, but due to the second Intifada, it was decided to change the location to a venue midway between the UK and Israel. An Italian member of OFEK helped facilitate the choice of venue in Italy and the decision to hold the conference there was welcomed by the Italian Group Relations people.

Boundaries and their political meanings in the Belgirate Conference

The Belgirate Conference was open to anyone who: (a) had previously taken up at least one conference staff role (administrative, consultative or directorial); and (b) had attended conferences that were based on the Tavistock-Leicester model. These two elements had political and conceptual meanings. It established the Tavistock-Leicester model of Group Relations conferences (GRCs) as the proto-type Group Relations conference, as distinct from other types of experiential conferences. This forced individuals and Group Relations organisations around the globe to face questions of identity, as well as allegiance to the Tavistock-Leicester GRC model. The two conditions of membership mentioned above made explicit a defin-ition of the boundary of inclusion and exclusion around the Belgirate Conference and by extension around the international Group Relations network. Eligibility criteria, i.e. having had a previous con-ference staff role, were boundary conditions that were actively implemented in more than one case by the management. These decisions helped preserve the primary task of the conference: not learning about GRCs, even though this was an important by-product for many participants, but rather reviewing and exploring the theory and practice of GRCs from within a boundary, termed in the conference the 'Group Relations network'.

Data

Invitations to the conference were sent to all Group Relations organ-isations and other organisations sponsoring GRCs around the world, about 30 in all. These organisations responded positively to our request, agreed to identify their members who had previously taken up staff roles in Group Relations conferences and forward our invitations on to them. Applications were received from individuals from 20 organisations. Fifty-two participants attended the confer-ence and their distributions reveal meaningful data about the characterisation and political dynamics of the Group Relations net-work. For example, participants came from 11 countries (Australia, Denmark, Finland, Germany, Israel, Italy, Netherlands, Spain, Sweden, UK and USA). Significant by their absence were representa-tives from France who, despite being very active in initiating and producing experiential conferences on authority and leadership, declared that they no longer considered themselves as part of the international Tavistock-Leicester Group Relations network.

Of interest here is that participants identified themselves as members of 19 different Group Relations organisations, indicating a sense of belonging that is served by their membership of Group Relations organisations. There were instances where people did not reveal any association with a Group Relations organisation; and there were some statements of mixed allegiances that perhaps reflected complex and ambivalent relationships towards Group Relations work and towards individuals' local Group Relations organisations.

Gender, age and role distributions

Thirty-two females and 20 males attended the conference. Forty-nine out of the 52 were over 40 years old; 34 were above 50.

Previous conference roles

Twenty participants had previously taken up director and other roles; 26 had been in consultant roles and six had been in administrator role only. We were struck by the number of people who had been in administrator role, pointing to the importance that this role plays in Group Relations conferences.

Structure and design of the Belgirate Conference

Our basic assumptions with regard to the work of exploring the various elements of the primary task of the conference, rested upon the existence of an international network of Group Relations organisations and individuals engaged in Group Relations work. These influence and are influenced by each other, nationally and internationally, consciously and unconsciously. We were keen to design a conference that would contain an international dimension through the presentation of papers by members of the network, representing different aspects of the international scene – nationality, religion, geography, gender and race. Colleagues from seven countries were invited to present their work on a variety of applications of Group Relations conferences. There were five major elements in the conference; each dealing with one aspect of the primary task. The design involved moving progressively from more structured events to less structured and more experiential ones.

1. *Theory of Group Relations*: Theory of Group Relations was delivered via a keynote lecture entitled: 'Learning from Experience and the Experience of Learning in Group Relations Conferences'. The lecture was followed by small group discussions. Allocation to groups was done by the conference management and reflected a more structured intent.
2. *Structure and Design of Group Relations Conferences*: this topic was explored via a keynote lecture entitled: 'Structure and Design of Group Relations Conferences: Issues and Dilemmas'. The lecture was followed by small group discussions on pre-assigned topics (Small Study Groups, Large Study Groups, Institutional Event, Review and Application Groups and Staff Meetings).
3. *Taking up Roles in Group Relations Conferences*: this event was experiential in which the participants explored the impact of various identity-related variables, such as nationality, religion, geography, gender and race, on taking up roles in Group Relations conferences. The process of exploration in this event relied on 'here and now' experiences of the conference itself to further the work of the event, i.e. the groups that formed engaged with each other in their representations of the different variables. The groups worked on their tasks by using the conference Directorate (the two managers and the two administrators) for consultation and for engagement, via dialogue and interviews.
4. *Application*: exploring the nature of application of Group Relations conferences was achieved through eight parallel presentations by participants of their own work followed by a plenary meeting
5. The conference programme included a space first thing each morning for 'morning reflections' in which dream material emerged to shed light on important dynamics of the conference.

Roles in the conference

The Directorate comprised managers and administrators. In addition to the lecturers and presenters of papers, other roles included chairs and convenors of the different sessions and these roles were distributed among the participants. Altogether, 21 participants held a variety of roles in the conference. This design, and the fact that we designated ourselves as 'managers' and not 'directors', reflected our view that the conference should constitute a meeting of colleagues to pursue a common task. Additionally, we wished to distinguish this conference from a regular Group Relations conference. We hoped to produce a blend of traditional scientific and experiential modes of working that would enable creative learning to take place and simultaneously contain the dynamics that might emerge. During the design phase of the conference, we were anxious because of the conference's unique conception. Mixed traditional scientific and experiential methods of work usually produce complexity and tension. The challenge was to find a creative and containing balance.

Emergent metaphors, themes and issues

Chicken soup

This metaphor appeared in a dream in the first 'morning reflections' event. Associations presented included: what kind of 'soup' did the conference organisers prepare for the participants? Some participants felt 'thrown into the soup'. The conference was experienced as a 'Jewish soup'. Associations to the dream concerned the nature of the conference and the relatedness between the participants and the conference. Chicken soup is traditionally regarded as the 'Jewish medicine' for all problems, administered by an all-loving Jewish mother. Did the conference represent health-giving regenerative chicken soup or the more negative aspects of benign coercion, submergence in a 'Jewish soup/conference', suggesting loss of autonomy, control by the ubiquitous Jewish mother and guilt for rejecting life-giving sustenance?

Criticism of the structure

Participants felt forced into a structure that did not always feel productive. People were faced by the painful realisation that they had made a choice to join something about which they had only vague notions. This made them feel entrapped and confronted by their responsibilities for having decided to participate, followed by an internal struggle, on the one hand, to make the best of their experiences, or on the other, to remain locked in opposition. These two lines of engagement with the conference, both personal and in relation to institutional identity, persisted almost until the end of the conference.

London Underground map

This concerned the London Transport Underground map. The features of a good design are simplicity and applicability. 'Underground' competition and rivalry in the Group Relations network were forced into the open. This metaphor emerged in relation to the discussion around the design of this conference, in particular, and Group Relations conferences generally: what is innovation and what is conservative tradition? The metaphor seemed to represent the durability of the Tavistock-Leicester model of Group Relations conferences insofar as they contain the two basic elements of good design – simplicity and flexibility. It was posited that the actual London Transport Underground map of 1931 was the first to incorporate diagrammatic principles of using only vertical, horizontal and 45° lines even though the spatial relationships between stations on the map did not match reality on the ground. As new lines were developed over the years they were easily slotted into the existing design. This model of underground map-making was adopted by about 150 underground systems throughout the world. This metaphor was powerfully present in the conference around questions of whether the Tavistock-Leicester model was actually out of date or whether it contained the basic elements from which adaptations and new learning events could be built. This metaphor reverberated throughout the conference, ushering the conference into the underground/hidden or unconscious dynamics of the Group Relations network. Thus for example: which countries and Group Relations organisations now held the mantle of leadership and innovation?

The institution of Group Relations 'in the mind'

The Belgirate Conference provided an opportunity for map building of the Group Relations network, of the institution of Group Relations that individuals and Group Relations organisations hold in their minds. Maps are only representations of reality, not reality itself, but at the same time, without maps, adaptations to reality cannot be made. In this respect, the Belgirate Conference started the process of articulating and drawing the map, both of the institution of Group Relations with its more obvious overt and conscious elements, and the unconscious elements of relationships and relatedness among its various 'stations' or international Group Relations organisations.

'Is the friend dead or alive?'

A participant dreamed of a friend lying down in a house, apparently suffering a heart attack. The dreamer is worried, rushes outside to hail an ambulance but fails to find one. He comes back inside to find the friend is up and well.

The dream may have touched on the internal process of the conference with the management under attack and a fear that management, and therefore, the conference, could be fatally damaged. The dream was presented after a day of continuous attack on the management and represented the well-known phenomenon of management being both an object of continuous destructive attack and needing to be protected and preserved. The attacks on the management were at times difficult to contain and to manage. We were familiar with this phenomenon through our work in GRCs. Yet, this conference was unique, in that we had to manage a process involving colleagues, many of them our compatriots and good friends. We had to face situations suffused with the dialectic of support and competition, of envy and of gratitude. The dream may have represented unconscious attempts to manage those impulses simultaneously.

At another level, the dream may have represented the joint and shared ambivalent relationship towards the Tavistock-Leicester Group Relations conference model, by asserting that the model was outdated, conservative, authoritarian and controlling. On the other hand, anxiety about the continued existence of Group Relations led to strenuous efforts to preserve it. The dream may have represented the perennial dilemma: is the model dead or dying? Or is it alive and well?

Eric Miller's death and the issue of authority in the Group Relations world

Eric Miller headed the Tavistock Institute's Group Relations Programme for over 30 years and came to symbolise both the theoretical underpinnings and the practical design and structure of the Leicester model. The issue of professional authority in the Group Relations world had been exposed by his death. One reference to this question was pointedly made by suggesting that there was 'no longer a Pope, only two Chief Rabbis'. On one level, this statement obviously referred to the two Jewish managers of the conference who took leadership by mounting this conference. But, on another level, the implication was that from here on there would be no single great man running the Group Relations world, but rather joint or cooperative leadership. However, the question of leadership is usually accompanied by competition. Now that there is no 'Pope', would the 'sons' fight among themselves for leadership, for power and influence?

'Birth order'

In aspiring for leadership, 'birth order' i.e. dates of establishment of different Group Relations organisations, was manifested powerfully in the role-taking event, where all the American AKRI participants 'found' themselves in one group, 'not by design', they claimed. Should the 'firstborn' (AKRI) be regarded as the natural inheritors of the authority and leadership mantle? Feelings were consequently aroused because a relatively 'new-born' organisation, viz. OFEK, took its own authority to team up with the Tavistock Institute and conceptualise, establish and run this conference. Did the personal, ethnic, mutual experiences of the two conferences managers play a part in forming the basis of this particular partnership? Though these were important factors in forging this relationship, another significant factor might have been related to the nature of the relationship that was developed and maintained between the Tavistock Institute and OFEK, viz. the loyalty that the two organisations held for each other over the years, that moved from dependency to reciprocity and interdependence. This hypothesis touches on interesting historical developments of the various offspring Group Relations organisations in relation to the 'parent' Tavistock Institute organisation.

Being 'chosen'

A major element concerning involvement in role-taking was the idea of being 'chosen', which appeared to be more significant than variables like gender, religion and profession. It emerged that for many participants, perhaps all, becoming a staff member in a conference depended upon 'being chosen', either by a director or by a sponsoring institution. In addition to the potentially painful narcissistic issues involved in being chosen or excluded, were questions of unhealthy dependency, the degree of freedom in the work, genuineness and authenticity. Failing to attend to these dynamics could lead to corruption of the learning process, implying that Group Relations, like every other human endeavour, has the seeds of its own destruction within it. Moreover, the notion of being 'chosen' can be played out in the arena of organisational relationships in terms of which organisations are chosen by other organisations for joint ventures, a dynamic that was powerfully present in this conference.

The nature of staff meetings

In order to explore various dilemmas regarding structure and design of GRCs, the participants were asked to divide into various groups representing major GRC elements – Small Study Groups, Large Study Groups, Inter-Group Event, Institutional Event, Review and Application Groups and Staff Meetings. The Staff-Meeting-group attracted the largest number of participants (20); the other groups attracted between four and 12. It was clear that the nature of staff meetings is a major undiscussed element in GRCs. Questions were raised regarding the primary task of staff meetings, the need to keep firm time boundaries, as in other conference meetings, and the kind of work that needs doing. It was clear that the nature of staff meetings is relatively unexplored territory. The large interest in the 'Staff-Meetings' group suggests a need for further work on this issue.

Authority lies within the network

The question of how this conference came into being reverberated throughout the conference. It was only towards the end of the conference that it was fully understood that the organisers of the Belgirate Conference took their own authority and made the conference self-authorising, although they were strongly supported by their organisations, OFEK and the Tavistock Institute, by virtue of the roles they held in them. This creative self-authorising process was acknowledged by the participants, not from a competitive position, but from the realisation of the power of an idea. It was realised that the authority to act in the arena of world Group Relations would not come from 'above', but henceforth would lie within the network.

Concluding thoughts

Deciding to hold the Belgirate Conference along the lines discussed in this paper has shaped the emergence of a Group Relations network with its own authority, and where authority no longer lies with a single individual or a single organisation. The initiative leading to the formation of the conference depended on taking leadership in the relatively undefined world of Group Relations. The large number of participants from many countries made this initiative a success. It reflects the need – supported by participants at the aftermath of the conference – for the development of more conferences of this kind.

Part I

Structure, design and learning in Group Relations Conferences

The opening phase of the Belgirate Conference was devoted to the theme of Structure, Design and Learning in Group Relations conferences. Olya Khaleelee and Mira Erlich-Ginor, the two keynote speakers, offered perspectives that are central to the questions of this book: into what realm of learning do Group Relations conferences fall? That Group Relations conference learning is experiential is axiomatic; but both authors penetrate deeper in their study of *learning from experience and experience of learning* and how *structure and design* allows learning to take place.

Clearly, for both authors, the influence of Eric Miller, a key figure in the history of Group Relations, is profoundly present. While they both acknowledge his role in their personal and professional development, they proceed from that position to question the 'institutionalising tendencies' of Group Relations conferences and the prospect that goes with institutionalisation – a decline in the capacity to be surprised and to learn, suggesting that new emotional learning can be achieved only by ceasing to rely on learning already achieved.

Each author's paper has a distinctive cultural feel – British and Israeli – yet both reflect on the benefits of Group Relations experiential learning, on the dangers of institutionalisation and on the need for innovation.

Olya Khaleelee's and Mira Erlich-Ginor's papers attest a fundamental hypothesis that learning in and of Group Relations conferences comes from the deliberate raising of anxiety (even fear), not its alleviation. Defensiveness against anxiety of the unknown is dealt with in numerous ways, principally by projecting omniscience and omnipotence into leaders, depending on them to provide us with protection. Both authors develop links between these psychic processes and experiences of group life in Group Relations conferences. Olya Khaleelee's paper takes that further in descriptions of her work

15

with organisations and Mira Erlich Ginor shares her conference experiences and dilemmas about the impact of structure and design on learning.

Both authors emphasize the value of exercising personal authority that is an intrinsic pillar of Group Relations tradition, theory and ideals. Moreover, it is suggested implicitly that Group Relations theory and practice can contribute to responsible 'taking up and exercising national and global authority', respecting task and boundary, where intervention strategies and transformations might happen as a result of learning from experience.

CHAPTER ONE

Learning from experience and the experience of learning in Group Relations Conferences

Olya Khaleelee

My immediate thought when invited to give this keynote paper was that, had Eric Miller been alive, he would probably have been standing here instead of me. So, whilst I was explicitly invited here in my own right, I also feel that I am representing Eric's absence as well as the powerful presence of his work and influence, which lives on in me and I am sure, in many of you. He taught us well.

When I started to write this paper I thought first about my own ways of learning, about what they meant to me and what it was about them that made them different from each other. There are three relevant modes of learning that I identified.

The first was learning by rote, which some of us did a lot of at school. Rote learning is useful because with a snap of your fingers you can produce the answer to 9×8! Memorising your multiplication tables and the formula for long division are of lifelong use. Unfortunately this kind of learning is limited.

My second mode of learning was learning by telling, mostly gained from lectures and seminars in educational institutions. This kind of learning did require my thinking capacity, my critical faculties. It involved more than stimulus and response, it challenged and broadened my mind and provided scope for associating to ideas. However, the impact of this kind of learning seemed largely confined to intellectual development.

The third kind of learning is learning by experience, falling into two parts. The first is to do with mastering certain 'motor' skills, such as riding a bike, learning to swim, learning to roller skate, where you can only be taught so much. In the end, you have to learn by doing, by being 'thrown in at the deep end', and once skills like that are mastered, they remain with you forever.

The second part of learning by experience is to do with being in a setting with enough uncertainty to produce emotional growth and the opportunity to mature. The gap year between school and university is a wonderful example of just such an opportunity. In another way, so is a personal psychoanalysis or participation in a Group Relations conference.

Whilst all these modes of learning require the mastery of anxiety, it is only in these last examples that anxiety is specifically mobilised in order to learn. Perhaps it is this that makes the experiences particularly powerful and intense.

This chapter falls naturally into three parts: first, learning by experience and the experience of learning as a member in Group Relations conferences; second, learning by experience and the experience of learning as a staff member (and director); and third, how those experiences are applied to organisational life outside. I want to say a little about each of these.

Learning by experience as a member

Thinking about learning by experience re-evoked memories of my own first attendance at a Group Relations conference. In 1973 I was invited to work on a change project led by my colleague and friend, Andrew Szmidla, a very creative psychologist. He had joined a multi-national company then engaged in a process of rapid change and acquisition, to be the Managing Director's special Advisor on Change. His responsibilities were to identify areas where change was required and develop strategies to bring them about. A particular acquisition was causing concern to top management and, with the Managing Director's encouragement, Andrew met the most recently appointed general manager.

With him as his initial client Andrew invited me to work with him as an internal consultant, which was both a terrifying and exciting prospect and, in itself became a profound learning experience, which I will say more about in thinking about application.

Almost the first thing we did was to attend the 1973 Leicester Conference, which was directed by Pierre Turquet. I confess I could make no sense of the experience at all, bar learning about how help-less and dependent I felt, particularly on management. My main memory is of having had to manage very high levels of anxiety and uncertainty, which were almost paralysing. I am not sure that I learnt anything specific from that experience but it did put me strongly in touch with my guts and made me consider that my feel-ings were a relevant source of data when taking up my internal consulting roles at work.

I returned to my second Leicester Conference in 1976, which was an entirely different experience. In the intervening three years, my own life had been rather turbulent but, in collaboration firstly with Andrew, and later with Eric, who came in to work with us as our external consultant, I had begun to understand the concept of sys-tems thinking, was very taken by the idea of the unconscious at group and organisational levels and had located my own authority. I was raring to use it! Thus, going to the Leicester Conference in 1976 was an exhilarating experience of testing myself out and exercising my authority. I had a wonderful time, learnt an enormous amount about my own capacities and resilience, and came away feeling completely omnipotent. Not necessarily a good state to be in when working as an internal consultant!

So, in considering the process of learning from experience, I began to think about these two experiences as a member and what it was that differentiated them. Firstly, I could say that in the 3 years between the two experiences I had probably matured. Certainly the intervening time had presented me with many situations of high uncertainty and considerable anxiety, both personally and profes-sionally, that I had learnt to manage and which had stretched me, it felt almost in a physical as well as a psychological sense. Secondly, my heightened self-awareness and feeling of power were balanced by a sense of responsibility – I now had to use what I had learned in the service of the task. Thirdly, I was working with colleagues who provided important support through their capacity to think and reflect on our joint work. Although very uncertain, it was at the same time a containing environment.

Since then, in my role as a corporate psychologist working with senior managers on developmental issues and career strategy, I have repeatedly had confirmation that it is generally difficult life experiences – those that generate anxiety and uncertainty – that help the individual to develop their 'emotional intelligence', in other words, to mature at an emotional level and to find their personal authority. But the level of difficulty needs to be experienced as manageable rather than overwhelming so that it is not traumatising or paralysing. There needs to be some mitigating balance so that the event becomes one of growth and not a regressive experience.

I considered whether what happens in these situations is that 'emotional intelligence' is mobilised and stretched as well as intellectual capacity and the two – often kept apart – can be integrated. And I wondered whether the reason some people gain more from and make more sense of conference experiences than others is because, at the time of their attendance, they have within them a better balance between their intellectual capacity, to which great attention is paid during the formative years, and the level of their 'emotional intelligence' which is frequently neglected. The exceptions are those who have had some therapy or analysis, or who have experienced well enough early nurture, to enable their 'emotional intelligence' to develop in balance with their intellectual capacity. This emotional capacity is, in my view, key to being able to contain and manage anxiety and uncertainty and relates to the capacity to move from the paranoid-schizoid to the depressive position.

Some of the foregoing applied to me, so I suspect that the difference in my capacity to learn between attending these two Leicester experiences was to do firstly, with a maturing process linked to my own developing capacity to manage my anxieties and secondly, with the effectiveness of the containment provided by staff at the conference.

This brings to mind the notion of the 'anxious edge', which could be the boundary at which learning occurs. Miller (1983) points out that creativity always carries within it the potential for destructiveness. The Group Relations conference provides an opportunity for new ways of looking at the world, new meanings and new ways of doing things, all of which are potentially creative. He points out that the opportunities to learn threaten to destroy some sense of 'shared reality' about how the world works and on this 'shared reality' are posited many assumptions about how things should be done. The threat generates anxiety and resistance, the anxiety partly being to do with an uncertainty about distinguishing creative and destructive impulses inside oneself. This could be seen as the anxious edge at which learning occurs.

So, a precipitating factor in the generation of anxiety and the possibility of learning by experience, is of feeling surprised out of these normal ways of thinking and being. As a conference member with the normal past experience of much learning by telling, a conference experience studying the 'here and now' is unfamiliar, elusive and initially, at least, deskilling. There is also a disjunction between members who see themselves as individuals, and consulting staff, who interpret their behaviour in terms of the group. This challenge of assumptions throws the member's identity into the air, calling into question the sense of self and the boundary between self and other (Miller, 1989, p.25).

Palmer (1979), drawing on a paper by Bateson (1973) elaborates three levels of learning. The first is where members identify and label some of the unusual things they have experienced, but they do it from the perspective of the 'observing ego'. The second level goes beyond observation to conceptual change, as the experience changes the way in which the member thinks about the world; and the third level seems to involve a degree of internal restructuring in terms of one's personality.

Palmer says 'It is something different from being knowledgeable about one's own character, in the manner of those who justify their behaviour with statements like: "Well you see, I am a very dependent (obsessive, paranoid, untidy) person". The experience of level 3 learning is the experience of becoming responsible for one's dependence (obsessiveness, paranoia, untidiness) as something one is, and is doing'.

Here we can see the shift from a defensive paranoid-schizoid mode to the more depressive position of taking authority and responsibility for uncomfortable elements within oneself. In support of this notion, Laurence Gould pointed out to me in a recent e-mail conversation, that this shift also brings with it both another level of anxiety and the burden of taking responsibility for things it is much easier to disown. He said: 'In this sense the experience of learning is a highly ambivalent emotional mixture of potency and pleasure, but also of ambivalence and hatred, since once having learned something, one has to take full responsibility for using it constructively. Who the hell wants to know some things about oneself and take responsibility for them? The loss of righteous indignation and rage is indeed a profound psychic loss! This is of course the most general aspect of resistance . . . in a Group Relations conference . . .'. It is also the major loss of moving from a paranoid schizoid to a depressive position.

Learning by experience as a staff member

As a staff member one's task is to provide opportunities for members to learn from experiences in the conference. However, looking at the literature and at my own experience as staff member makes it clear that providing opportunities for members necessitates our capacity to learn by our experiences, and especially being able to manage the anxieties involved in such learning.

Gosling (1981) addressed the question of surprise in the capacity to learn from a theoretical perspective. He listed various characteristics of very small groups, distinguishing them from small groups. He went on to identify 'only four clusters of past experience from which psychological models appear to be drawn.' These were first, the Confessional, representing the search for intimacy; second, the Family, representing something pleasurable often at variance with actual experiences of family life; third, Negotiation – involving the regulation of individual differences around questions of political power, commercial negotiations, personal values and fourth, the Balloon or Lifeboat – 'a balloon in which someone has got to be jettisoned and who is it going to be?'. He then went on to recount a further experience of consulting to a very small group within a Leicester Conference, this time for Training Group members in which the processes were quite different. 'What I thought I had learned so far seemed to have only the vaguest relevance'.

He pointed out how quickly a formulation, concept or theory loses its enabling quality and becomes a barrier to the possibility of making further observations. He links this to his experience as an analyst of always having to rediscover anew the theory of the Oedipus complex, as if it must 'lie just on the boundary of what I must repress and what I must acknowledge. The instability of what is known, or thought to be known, seems to be required if it is to be rediscovered repeatedly, always in a new setting and so always for the first time. . . . It is as if learning always has to take place on the edge of exasperation' (p.645)

Eric Miller (1989, p. 21) also commented on how, as a director, after many years' experience, he gradually began to lose his capacity to be surprised and how he had to struggle against becoming institutionalised. He recognised also the pressures from members and staff to provide such containment that they could also avoid surprise. He noted 'that members will often learn more from an inexperienced staff member, who is constantly confronted with the unfamiliar and lacks the repertoire of tried and tested responses'.

This brings sharply to mind a personal experience, when I had begun to work as a young staff member in conferences. It was the opening plenary of a short non-residential Group Relations conference that Eric Miller was directing with a small staff group. He welcomed participants and spoke at some length about the nature of authority, leadership and the task of the conference. I particularly remember his voice, deep, melodious and increasingly soothing. Suddenly, he ended his opening remarks, but it felt too as if he suddenly stopped speaking. There was an almost visible shock reaction (which the staff also experienced) as though the dependency generated in an almost parental way from the opening, had suddenly been ripped away, leaving a no-man's land of uncertainty for all of us. Members looked at each other not knowing what to do and staff tried hard not to look at each other! Some on the front row smiled, I thought as a reaction formation to the anxiety that was generated by this loss of basic assumption dependency. Thus began a very useful learning experience for staff and members alike.

Thinking about anxiety as a primary factor in learning by experience and being very much at the 'anxious edge' in writing this paper, made me turn to Bion, (1961) who draws attention to the powerful feelings inherent in group process, reminding us that 'anxiety, fear, hate, love, all . . . exist in each basic-assumption group. The modification that feelings suffer in combination in the respective basic-assumption group may arise because the "cement", so to speak, that joined them to each other is guilt and depression in the dependent group, Messianic hope in the pairing group, anger and hate in the fight-flight group'. Primitive anxiety is present in all of them, impelling the group to take defensive action.

In relation to conferences, Rice (1965, p.44) also talks about anxiety in the context of leadership and decision-making – 'anxiety about the amount and quality of information available on which the decision has to be based, anxiety about the capacity to make the decision, and anxiety after it has been made while waiting for its consequences'. This is similar to Jaques' (1976) concept of the time span of discretion, whereby the capacity of the leader to hold and implement his or her vision, depends on the ability to manage the uncertainty of not knowing the outcome of decisions made, which could have a time span of up to 30 years. From my perspective as a corporate psychologist, this ability is directly related to the level of 'emotional intelligence' of the individual.

Rice points out that it is unlikely that much can be learned about anxiety without the learners becoming anxious and that 'the problem of the conference institution is not . . . to avoid anxiety, but to provide opportunities to examine its effect on behaviour and to learn ways of dealing with it, so that the outcome is constructive'. Because the capacity to tolerate anxiety differs between individuals, there is the technical problem of providing opportunities to learn in an individual way and at one's own pace.

He also points out how important it is that staff should also be anxious at some points in a conference in order to be fulfilling their roles appropriately, containing, understanding and learning from their own anxieties in order to be able to provide opportunities for conference members to learn. In this way it is also part of the role of staff to exercise dependable leadership for members through knowing what they are doing and carrying it out competently. Certainly, staff were put closely in touch with their anxieties in the example I mentioned above when Eric Miller stopped speaking.

In another conference where I was a young staff member, I recall being so paralysed by the end of an opening plenary that I feared I would not be able to get up and leave the room at the time boundary. There was even a point at which my body felt so rigid that I thought I might not stay upright and might fall sideways on to the staff member next to me. This happened to me on a few occasions early in my 'Group Relations career' and, as well as being terrified by the experience, I was very puzzled about what it meant. Eventually I came with help to the hypothesis that I was experiencing massive envy from the participants, which, together with my own fright, was making me seize up and preventing me from working. Once I had grasped this, I was able to offer myself the hypothesis when it happened and work with it openly. But this experience, from which I learnt a great deal, was extremely powerful and frightening in its intensity. It has, however, been very useful since.

Applying learning experiences in Group Relations conferences to the outside world

Finally, I would like to give two examples where the learning from Group Relations conferences was applied very effectively to other institutions. The first links back to the work Andrew Szmidla and I carried out as internal consultants back in the 1970s. This was, unusually, a direct application of the Group Relations model to organisational change. The client system was a merged organisation engaged in the manufacture of a specialist product, comprising subsystems that had previously been in competition in the market. Each had held 30% of the market, but post-merger the potential market share of 60% had dropped markedly, labour turnover rose and many signs of organisational distress were in evidence.

The sales force was removed from the organisation and merged with a general divisional sales force with little knowledge of this particular product. The diagnosis of this organisation's problems indicated that it was suffering from a loss of identity generated by the merger – involving a part of the outside world being forced in – and by the loss of an important boundary function, exercised through the sales force – involving a part of the inner world being removed. Our hypothesis was that in losing one of its main boundary controls – the sales force – this organisation was suffering from fragmentation, with employees falling back on more meaningful inner groups and sub-groups that could provide the security and meaning that was otherwise absent.

With the help of our external consultant, Eric Miller, we designed an intervention. Our aim was to try and bring about a re-integration of the organisation by giving employees an opportunity to examine the beliefs, assumptions, myths and attitudes that underlay current working relationships. In other words, we aimed to modify the splitting, projection and other processes taking place and to rebuild the main boundary by rebuilding the internal connectedness of the organisation. Miller later wrote about the first phase of this project (1977).

The whole management – 126 employees – including the General Manager – participated in the programme, which was divided into three parts. The first was a series of group meetings – 9 groups met for 1½ hours a week for 10 weeks. The aim was to explore relationships between group members, the processes going on in the groups and what these might mean. Each group had 14 members from different levels of management; they worked, as one might at a Leicester Conference, with a consultant who offered hypotheses about processes going on in the group.

The second phase of the programme focused on what was going on between groups. Two weekends were spent at the Head Office staff college exploring inter-group processes. One significant theme was the absence of authority in any of the groups that formed. Many of the groups felt that real authority was located in the top management group, some of whom found themselves together. The few members who dared to go and see what was happening to them, found them in total disarray. Their belief was that the real authority resided in Head Office. Although this part of the programme did not ask participants to look specifically at what was going on in the system, the actual behaviour of the groups provided a very clear mirror of what in fact was going on, and it became increasingly clear to the participants both what they were doing to their own top management – thereby creating a 'them and us' situation – and what top management was doing to Head Office.

Insights derived from these experiences of splitting and projection were taken back into the organisation and worked through in the small group configurations, now essentially functioning as application groups, looking at how these experiences related to people's roles.

Finally, a third phase of the programme began, which was a series of large group meetings where the whole of management met together. The meetings aimed to look at the total system and how it related to its environment – customers, suppliers, the community – as an entity. An interim review of the state of the organisation seemed to indicate that it was in transition, holding on to a past that now appeared rosier than it actually was but with some movement to creating a better present.

From this initial input developed what was already coming to be called the People Programme – an opportunity for employees to work through some of the trauma of the acquisition and merger and to begin to take back the authority projected into Head Office.

Within the People Programme, members of the organisation found additional or alternative ways of relating to each other. Other groups began to emerge. The group of project engineers who had come together to look at the unsatisfactory working situation in the Engineering Department, were, a year later, running a mini People Programme for other employees in the department. Perhaps a more striking example of the use of personal authority was the setting up of a group for the apprentices, who felt they were used as cheap labour and were not receiving appropriate training; they came together to take steps to remedy the situation and were successful.

One of the key things that emerged from this intervention was that employees in this organisation, having previously felt completely taken over and helpless to manage themselves in role, had found ways of using their own authority anew. This capacity strengthened as the organisation as a whole was gradually able to move from a fragmented to an integrated state. What was important was the capacity to manage both internal and external boundaries. Andrew Szmidla recently pointed out to me that this was one of the key learning points from the Leicester Conference model: having a way of representing the process through concepts like boundary. The notion of crossing the boundary, how you manage to do this, the question of how permeable it is and whether it is there at all were all major issues.

There were many other developments both conceptually and practically. From a business point of view, the People Programme represented an alternative value system to that of the organisation as a whole and had helped it to change its position and its relationship to other product groups in the division. Profits rose, confidence increased, labour turnover halved, it seemed to have gained a better sense of identity and, according to the results of a later survey, a more realistic orientation to the outside world. Our client had gone from being a poor performer to being a successful business.

Looking conceptually at our intervention strategy and the transformations our client organisation has undergone, one can see the impact of learning from experience. In this case a whole organisation – not only individuals and groups – had to manage its anxiety of learning from experience. It was our role to provide a structure of intervention that will be containing enough not only to provide opportunities to 'learn from experiences', but also to enable individuals, groups and the organisation as a whole to have an 'experience of learning' of its underlying dynamics.

The second example was to do with my corporate work in a multinational beverages company. My current work partner, Ralph Woolf, and I had carried out psychological assessments on the country managers who reported to the regional Managing Director, an Argentinian. He was based in Miami and the managers – themselves of many different nationalities – were located in various South American countries: Ecuador, Peru, Colombia, Argentina, Mexico and so on, developing the distribution networks in each country and the South American market generally. It became clear to the Managing Director that his team needed to perform more effectively. He was concerned that they tended to compete with each other rather than co-operate and there was tension both between them and with him.

He therefore organised a weekend for them at the staff college in the UK and he invited Ralph and me to design a workshop. The task was to develop more effective working relationships. Bearing in mind our own experiences from Group Relations conferences and the potential problems of dependency and transference, we designed a workshop in which the managing director managed the boundary both at the beginning and the end, thus providing the overall containment. The aim here was to support his authority and, because of the brevity of this workshop, to minimise dependency by him and his team on us.

He began by presenting his strategy for the next three years. He explicitly delegated authority to us to provide an input for the team. I gave a lecture on Klein, Bion and basic assumption group behaviour. The team was then asked to work on the issues concerning them, as a result of how the strategy would impact on their roles as country managers and how they, comprising such a multi-cultural mix of people, could find ways to work more effectively together. Built into this discussion were 15-minute pause points in which they had to examine their own process, with Ralph and me consulting to them.

What emerged from this as a surprise to all those present, was that they were indeed highly competitive, but not in the way the MD had imagined. Their experience was that, because the MD was spending a great deal of time managing upwards, trying to cope with his own manager's anxieties about the performance of the South American region and therefore frequently absent at Head Office in London, he was not available enough to them. Their competitiveness stemmed not from their wish to have his job but from feeling neglected and abandoned by him, with concomitant feelings of anxiety. Once this was interpreted to the group and they could see that they shared a similar sense of uncertainty and isolation, they were able to co-operate warmly with each other and to talk very frankly with their boss.

Later, they shared their assessment reports with each other, discussed their similarities and differences, the impact of this on the culture of their part of the organisation and finally made decisions about more effective ways of working together, both horizontally with each other and with the MD. It was a very successful brief intervention, using inputs from Group Relations – especially those related to providing a structure to learn from the experience in the workshop – in order to explore existing anxieties and tensions and bring about change.

To conclude, I have attempted to demonstrate how the Group Relations model and its constructive use of anxiety, uncertainty and surprise, can be a powerful way of learning experientially, whether as a member of a conference, a staff member or in organisational life outside.

CHAPTER TWO

Structure and design of Group Relations Conferences

Issues and dilemmas

Mira Erlich-Ginor

A s I prepared this paper I thought: structure and design – yes, but there is also 'something else', that makes each confer-ence different, 'something else' that makes one conference 'magical' and another, 'just another conference'. Structure and design form the chess board and the rules of play, but the 'something else' forms the uniqueness of every game.

Two associations come to mind:

In the first association, it is the opening plenary session of one of the international *Authority, Leadership, and* . . . . . . conferences in Israel. The director has made his/her opening remarks; the adminis-trator adds some practical information. A deep and prolonged silence follows in the large hall. Someone asks: '*Why* do we sit like this? This is a strange and uncomfortable seating arrangement. By the way, my name is so and so and I suggest we move our chairs and form a circle'. In less than five minutes after the director has finished speaking, chairs are moved all over the place, there is noise and laughter and some members get knocked as chairs are passed over-head. A huge circle is formed, including the staff who have not moved their chairs but who have been pushed a little this way and that. A conference member sits next to a staff member with knees almost touching and entirely blocking his/her view. It is a large room and the circle of 50–60 people stretches from wall to wall. It is hard to see members at the far end and it is practically impossible to hear anyone.

This is typical of the beginning of an opening plenary in Israel. No matter who the director is – experienced or a novice, man or woman, a member will stand up and offer to improve the situation by changing the seating arrangements.

I now turn to the first German-Israeli Group Relations conference. The director finishes his speech; the administrator adds some practical information. A deep and prolonged silence falls on the large hall. Someone asks: 'Why do we sit like this? This is a strange and uncomfortable seating arrangement. I suggest we move our chairs and form a circle'. Chairs are moved all over the place, one member shouts at the top of his voice 'like sheep to slaughter'. The rest of the members ignore the remark and go on rearranging the seats. It is ten minutes after the director's speech, a huge circle has formed including the staff members who have not moved their chairs, etc. Two members, sitting together in what was the front row, have not moved. They have become an 'island' in the 'pool' that has formed. These two members, a German woman and a German man, had experienced an earlier OFEK Conference in Israel in which this scene had occurred.

At the closing plenary of these conferences, no one ever suggests changing the seating arrangements.

My second association is a Jewish story about a traveller who comes to a small village and is invited to stay for the Sabbath. He joins his host at synagogue. As they approach, he asks why everyone bows and passes through the synagogue door bent over uncomfortably. 'Is this not the way you enter your synagogue?' asks the host. 'I have never seen anything like this in all my travels', the visitor replies. Bewildered, the host approaches an old man in the synagogue, and asks him: 'Do you know the reason why we always enter the synagogue the way we do'? 'Yes', replies the old man, 'our community once had a synagogue that was destroyed by fire. Well, it had a low door . . .'.

Another image: 'Structure and Design' is the title on the empty page. What shall I write about? Rice in Learning for Leadership in 1965 and later, Eric Miller, in his 'Leicester Model' in 1989, said it all. Is there really anything to add? My distress grows as I go on reading and admiring the combination of their clarity, wisdom and humbleness. What has changed? What has been added?

I wondered why I felt this way. Is there nothing further to add? And if not, what does that mean? Are we 'bending our heads' without realizing that the 'new synagogue' now has a higher door? Do we go on doing the conferences in the way our 'ancestors' did? Without freedom to change, transform or create? Group Relations conferences are a great creation, providing in one week, a rare opportunity to learn and internalize understandings and to dialogue with unconscious processes, rather than act on them. Is there any need to change, transform and create?

The theme 'Structure and Design' allows for a variety of issues and dilemmas to be discussed. Each conference event offers interesting questions for thought. I have selected the following core issues:

- The 'Leicester' model: is it engraved in stone?
- Staff work: methodology and meaning
- Boundaries: their use and abuse

The 'Leicester' model: is it engraved in stone?

What is our relatedness to the 'Leicester' model? Do we 'hang' on to a design that was developed 34 years ago? Or do we have a brilliant piece of Group Relations architecture that we would be wise to keep? Is it a combination of these two positions? – possessing a good enough design to which we are indebted by our transferences and trapped by collective unconscious processes, so that any change feels like patricide – a taboo attack on the 'elders' and untouchable traditions of the tribe.

In order to explore these issues further, some definitions and differentiations are in order. Group Relations conferences are temporary training institutions designed to explore and study the tensions inherent in group life, using a method of experiential learning (Armstrong, 2002). The 'Leicester' model is a more specific entity, referring to conferences, residential or non-residential, that are defined by:

- their **design** that includes Large Study Groups (LSGs), Small Study Groups (SSGs), Inter-group Events (IGs), Institutional Events (IEs), Review and Application Groups (RAGs) and Plenaries.
- a **stance by staff** that is interpretive rather than facilitative.
- a focus that is on **the group as a whole** rather than on the individual.
- the conception of the conference as a *system*, a temporary learning organization, in which the parts are dynamically related to the whole, and in which the characteristics of the whole are not different from the dynamic characteristics of the parts.
- a **Primary Task** 'to study the exercise and nature of **authority and leadership**, through the interpersonal, inter-group and institutional relations that develop within the conference as an organization'.
- a structure and design that provides opportunities to experience and learn about unconscious processes in individuals, groups and organizations that pertain mainly to issues concerning authority and leadership.

Phenomena in the natural world go through endless chains of transformations and at times it is impossible to find the critical moment in which one stage changes into another. For Group Relations the question is: when does the 'Leicester' model change into an 'application', 'extension', 'transposition, or it becomes another model altogether? In his 'Leicester' model monograph, Eric Miller states: *'Despite some subsequent theoretical and technical developments, the Leicester Conference model of today was essentially established by the time Rice died in 1969'.* (Miller, 1989, p. 5).

Brief review

The first 'Leicester' Group Relations conference was organized by the University of Leicester and the Tavistock Institute of Human Relations in September 1957 and Eric Trist directed it. The title of the conference was *'Exploration in Group Relations: a residential conference'.* A detailed description of the conference appeared two years later in a book *Exploration in Group Relations* by Trist and Sofer (1959). The design of the first conference included a conference opening, small study groups (the main event), lectures, application groups, conference review (in the form of a plenary) and a follow-up event 6 months later.

The second 'Leicester' conference (1959) saw the introduction of the inter-group event and the large study group. In 1965 the inter-group event and the institutional event were separated into two events. By the time Rice died in 1969, the inter-group event was redefined with the primary task of *'studying the here-and-now of inter-Group Relations'*. The institutional event focused on studying the relationship and relatedness to the conference as an institution and the lectures were aborted. The different events were conceptualized and methodology established leading to a conference structure that we have today, starting with the most anxiety-arousing events (the small and large study groups), moving through to the ending of the SSGs and the LSG while simultaneously increasing the review and application groups with which the conference closes and the members cross the boundary back to the outside world. The inter-group event and the institutional event during the middle of the conference serve as the repository of the organizational unconscious (Rice, 1965, fig. 3, p. 30). So when we speak of the 'Leicester' model not changing, I refer to the design of specific events and to the entire 'programme as a process'.

The 1960s were an era of trial and error experimentation in Group Relations work. Events were redesigned, boundaries created, destroyed and recreated. There were full two-week conferences, in-house conferences, a four-month ongoing weekly conference (including SSG, AG, Lectures and IG), application work done in organizations in the Leicester area during the conference, reviews done by staff members. Many so-called 'mistakes' were made in playful, creative, risk-taking ways.

What has changed since 1969? Most changes are at the level of increased complexity in the conference structure by introducing more sub-systems and expanded authority relationships, e.g. introducing a structure with 3 sub-conferences – an 'A' sub-conference, a 'B' sub-conference and a Training Group for staff in training. In 2004, the three sub-conferences each had their own director in addition to having a director of the whole conference.

New events were introduced over the years. There was the praxis event, first held in Paris, 1978 (Director: Gordon Lawrence). In

1982, Gordon Lawrence introduced the social dreaming matrix into some Group Relations conferences, but not into the classical 'Leicester' conference; Irish Group Relations conferences have poetry reading sessions; the Grubb Institute uses a novel structure for the application group. I assume there are other new events that are not known to me, but my point is that relatively little innovation has been introduced into the basic Group Relations conference model. Why?

On the one hand, the basic model is a brilliant composition. The conference structure, its design as a process, its flow, the stance of the staff, all provide a unique and rare combination of elements that are worth keeping, forming a good 'container' for the primary task of the conference. However, I wonder whether there is sufficient experimentation within the Group Relations frame suggesting a fear of making 'mistakes'. 'A Zen master's life is a continuous mistake', goes the saying. Are we now too concerned about 'getting it right'? And if so, why? Eric Miller was worried about the 'institutionalization' of the Group Relations conference model. I would like to go further and suggest that the group relation community is in danger of treating the 'Leicester' conference design as a fetish object, ('custodians of the tradition' according to Miller), the fantasy being that any change will evoke retaliation. This fear of retaliation is problematic in all organizations, and more so in our own that sets out to observe and understand social processes rather then enact them.

What is the evidence for this statement? First, the fact that the design has changed so little. Second, is the inevitable reaction to proposed changes.

Every time I have introduced changes in a Group Relations conference, I have been met by a startled reluctance to engage with the proposed changes. It did not matter how small the proposed changes were. As an example, in the first Group Relations conference in Israel in 1987, most of the staff came from abroad. Only four staff were Israeli. All the conference members, bar one, were Israelis. I was one of the Israelis and it was my first experience of a Group Relations conference. The working language was English, which was logical because of the foreign staff. But my application group consisted of five Israeli members and an Israeli consultant and we continued to work in English. All our attempts to switch to Hebrew were met with interpretations. It made no sense to me. Nine years later, when I directed my first international conference I had the opportunity to solve my unease about the issue of language by introducing the following formulation: *'the conference working language is English, except in events in which all the assembled participants are Hebrew-speaking'*. This formulation has become our usual practice in OFEK, but at the time it was a source of unease and anxiety. The rationalization for wanting to keep things as they were is that language is a boundary and we were muddling the boundaries that could endanger our capacities for 'containment'.

A second example involves having a follow-up meeting after one of the Israeli conferences. People asked: 'aren't we attacking the notion of the temporariness of the conference?' 'What will be the meaning of "crossing the boundaries out of the conference"'? The view was that a follow-up meeting was an attack on the whole, on the unquestionable-ness of the conference. I had 'forgotten' that the first 'Leicester' conference in 1957 had a follow-up working day 6 months later. By 'forgetting', I had no sanctioned past to rely on and this gave us the opportunity to explore the anxiety around transgressing the imagined untouchable dimension of the structure. The introduction of a feedback form, of a list of relevant books and articles for members to read, or having a short meditation period for staff, were met with the same mixture of anxious resistance.

I am perhaps stating the obvious that Group Relations conferences are 'anxiety-producing enterprises', *'In every consulting room there ought to be two rather frightened people: the patient and the psychoanalyst. If they are not, one wonders why they are bothering to find out what everyone knows'* (Bion, W. R. (1973)). Likewise, in every event in a Group Relations conference there are X number of frightened people, for if they are all knowledgeable, why would they bother to be there? It is this sense of the 'unknown' that is defended against. Defensiveness seems easier for members to achieve. They can, and do, project omniscience onto the staff, embodied in the statement: 'we are guinea pigs in a well-controlled laboratory', reassuring themselves that all is known and under control. For the staff, holding to a known design serves as protection against the unknown, contributes to a defensive sense of sanctification, 'institutionalizing' or making a 'fetish' of the conference. The design and structure of the conference are the 'known', yet what happens in the conference is unique and therefore unknown. Neither members nor staff have been there before. All is new, unexpected and anxiety-provoking. Yesterday's interpretation has to give way to today's understanding and today's understanding too will fade away in the constant search for meaning. This is a difficult position to maintain. The wish 'to know' is strong. The spirit of exploration and play – 'to not know' – is under constant attack by the need to 'know'. Dependency on the known (the 'Leicester' model) is the social defence that our organizational culture mobilizes in the service of defence against anxieties intrinsic to the Group Relations consultant's task which is to facilitate 'learning, to explore without memory and desire', without ever fully 'knowing'.

Robert Gosling describes the dynamic of a very small study group (VSSG):

> There was much nostalgia for the raw experiences of the small study groups of yester-year. There was some pressure to demonstrate expertise in identifying some small group phenomena that had become familiar; . . . For my part, I had, by accepting a staff role in relation to the Training Group, come to put a premium on the fact that I had worked in two VSSGs before and so was more 'experienced' than most others. I was constantly hoping that some of the psychological models that had seemed to be fruitful in the past would turn out to be so again. . . . In fact the salient affective issues in the VSSG were of a depressive kind, in particular how one is one's own most dangerous saboteur and how one's public stance on the side of learning turns out to be a determination to repeat what one already knows and to learn as little that is new as possible. (Gosling, 1981, pp.160–1)

There is a built-in tension between 'knowing' and 'learning', between 'experimenting' and 'repeating'. This tension needs to be managed in the service of the staff and members' learning through their own experience. Have we rendered the 'Leicester' model a 'constant object' that has to be preserved? Like adolescents who need home to be there in order for them to explore the world, do we need 'Leicester' 'to be there' so that we can explore and innovate?

Staff work, methodology and meaning

Staff work is an intriguing aspect of Group Relations conferences. Staff work is part of the structure and design of the 'Leicester' model. There is variation in the way staff members take up their roles and the way the staff work as a group. Issues range from the invitation to be on the staff ('Why me?', 'Why not me?') through to working to task, the possibility of firing a staff member (as happened recently in France), or the director resigning (as almost happened in the first OFEK conference). I will focus on the 'working to task'. Being on the staff is a very intense situation in which a staff member is simultaneously a consultant, a person (man, woman, parent, child), a citizen and many other parameters, all of which are relevant in taking up the role of consultant in a Group Relations conference. For example, my gender is more often than not in the foreground. So is my Israeli-ness. My Jewish-ness is much less so. Two years ago, the 'Leicester' conference took place at the height of a wave of global and European anti-Semitism. My Jewish-ness came to the fore like never before, consciously and unconsciously. For example, I was the consultant of a group in the inter-group event that had no Jews. My Jewish-ness became foreground and my other characteristics became irrelevant.

Rice (1965, p. 49) says on being staff

> Essentially staff behaviour has to be 'professional'. By this I mean that members of staff have to accept full responsibility for what they say and how they behave . . . they have to be able to differentiate between person and role; between task and personal needs; and to recognize when their personal feelings are affecting their role performance. Recognize that making mistakes, as they will, is less important than the ability to recover from them. This means, in effect, that they strive always to remain in role, and that their behaviour, so far as they can control it, is appropriate to it. In events they do what the event defines they should do; on social occasions they behave socially. They do not, if they can help it, merge the one with the other. This does not mean that at meals, in the bar or on other social occasions they refuse to discuss the conference or its events if that is what interests those with whom they are talking – such behaviour would be antisocial.

This stance might come as a surprise to those of us whose stance is more removed and abstinent. The guidelines for staff work are clear: be in role when appropriate and leave it when not; keep a boundary between the professional and the personal; offer inter-pretations based on the 'here and now' and focused on the group level. Interpretations are working hypotheses based on evidence, so that they can be tested by the members. The reality of staff work is more diverse and interesting than this scheme suggests. I was struck by the differences in staff work at different conferences and in differ-ent countries. The behaviour, culture, body language, appropriate dress is heavily determined by cultural factors – the conference cul-ture and the general cultural context in which the conference takes place.

There is no agreed ethical code for staff behaviour in Group Rela-tions conferences. On the one hand, the staff group meets for a day before a conference and by noon the next day, a process begins that is a mixture of a 'jam' session and an orchestra with a director. Each staff member knows the instrument he or she is playing. Yet, there are differences in style and culture and in the conceptual under-standing of staff work and the theoretical background of the confer-ences. For example, the concept of projective identification is generally accepted as a working tool. Yet, one's use of the concept, the attribution of personal feelings to projective identification could lead to a mechanistic approach that creates a persecutory atmos-phere in the group. The way consultants interpret is related to their understanding of the human mind and their implicit theory of the unconscious. For example, using cryptic, oracular comments can be a defensive means of covering up insecurity, but they can also be based on an assumption that they communicate directly with the unconscious. The use of preaching-like statements can, likewise, emanate from a cycle of devaluation and retaliation between con-sultant and group, but it can be done intentionally as a pedagogic form of communication. Is it desirable to draw a boundary that marks certain interventions as acceptable and others as incompatible or abusive? In other words, should there be a code of ethics in this work? I think so.

The work of the staff as a group is also subject to wide variation. There are two positions. First, staff is a group within the conference institution. Because of parallel process, what goes on dynamically in the staff group is a major source of evidence for understanding the dynamics of the conference and its different sub-systems. This conceptualization parallels psychoanalytic work with the counter-transference and used wisely deepens our capacity for understanding.

Second, there is the view that *'staff . . . have to be able to differentiate between person and role; between task and personal needs, and to recognise when their personal feelings are affecting their role performance'*.

Staff group work could be a defence against 'being with' and 'for' the members. It could be a form of indulgence that stems from envy of the members having their conference. Some staff groups work past midnight, in turn becoming a small study group. On the other hand, some staff groups end early and this leaves them to do 'conference work' in informal and uncontained spaces.

Use and abuse of boundaries

Maintaining physical and psychical boundaries is central to the methodology of Group Relations conferences. The conferences 'take place' in the psychic territory of experience, in a potential space. This space is considered as existing between several boundaries – on the boundary between the inner world of feeling, fears, wishes and fantasies, and the 'real' world of roles and relationships, authority and accountability, between what is 'objectively perceived and what is subjectively conceived' (Winnicott, 1971), between the imagined and the concrete, between the personal and the social

> The third part of the life of a human being (besides the inside and outside), a part that we cannot ignore, is an intermediate area of experiencing, to which inner reality and external life both contribute. It is not challenged, because no claim is made on its behalf except that it shall exist as a resting-place for the individual engaged in the perpetual human task of keeping inner and outer reality separate yet interrelated. (Winnicott, 1971)

Time, territories, roles are strictly maintained in order to provide a 'secure enough container' that will enable the loosening of individual boundaries in the service of learning from experience. A 'good enough container' allows for play and risk-taking. But what is a 'good enough container'? The following vignette illustrates:

It is the early phase of the inter-group event, in an international Group Relations conference in Israel. A male Israeli member mentions to his newly-formed group that he has a gun. Anxiety rises immediately. Is his statement a disguised threat? And if so, of what? Suicide? Homicide? Group members are unsure. The statement about the gun was made at a time when no staff member was present, leaving the members with the problem of how to take up their authority. The group members urged the member with the gun to get rid of it. Notes appeared on the conference notice board saying 'remove the gun' 'we want no guns in the conference', and so on. The corridors filled with members with worried looks. Members reported the matter directly to staff.

The staff felt challenged. How should they deal with the situation? Were they in understanding mode? Was staff being pushed into action? Was this a situation where understanding and action converge? Is there such a thing as interpretation by action? Whose responsibility was it, anyhow? What is staff's role in cases like this? Boundaries were being challenged.

The situation should be put in context. The geo-political context is crucial for understanding this incident. The conference took place in Israel between the first and second intifada. The member was a 'settler' living in the 'territories'. To travel to and from home and work, and to the conference, he had to drive through hostile territory in which his life was endangered. His gun was for self-protection in case of a terrorist attack. This situation was unknown to members from abroad, for whom a gun signifies danger, a threat to *their* safety. It was the members from abroad who felt the anxiety and threat (perhaps on behalf of the Israelis).

At the staff meeting pieces of evidence and context are brought together. The counterpart of the Israeli-man-with-a-gun is a Hungarian-man-going-mad who is another source of worry for the Israeli members who act as hosts. The Hungarian's strange notes are placed on the notice board besides the notes about the gun.

After putting pieces of evidence together and forming an interpretation, the management meets and decides to approach the 'gunman' and explore further. No one has actually seen the gun. It may be a fantasy, though knowing the Israeli 'reality', it does not sound like a fantasy. The administrator talks to the member. He claims that he had wanted to place his gun in the hotel safe, but police orders prevented the hotel from accepting guns. The member says he decided to hold onto his gun. This, of course, did not explain why he had made such exhibitionistic use of the gun. He had had the gun for two days without mentioning it; he could have continued to remain silent about it until the end of the conference. An arrangement was worked out with the hotel office to put the gun away. The threat still remained and was used intentionally as way of checking boundaries and dynamics with members and with staff throughout the week. The gun became a means of communication for the conference and was used as a symbolic object with ever-changing meanings. The 'gun-man' felt secure enough to make his personal explorations. He learned a lot from this experimentation, so did we, learning by 'playing with fire'.

Boundaries are requisite for containment. They can be held, used and abused. They are abused when instead of containing anxiety they suffocate it, only to let it reappear in an unexpected place or time. Boundaries are abused when they become persecutory. Boundaries are a *process* though they tend to be too easily reified. There are conferences in which staff were persecuted because of ending a group session 30 seconds late. I see danger when the notion of boundaries as process turns concrete, so that 30 seconds is regarded as the difference between safety and imagined chaos. The reactions I described earlier in relation to the changes I had suggested came from an excessively concrete usage of the notion of boundaries. Yet boundaries can be fudged, can be violated and crossed. What is a good enough boundary? What is the appropriate level of flexibility we have to aspire to? These are questions that every conference has to negotiate. The story of the gun demonstrates working on the edge.

> If one were stranded on a desert isle, it would probably be better to find there a set of tools rather than, say, a finished house. (Pine, 1988, p. 593)

Group Relations are a set of tools that is seen too often as 'a finished house'. Tools are useful in creating potential spaces and in the service of generating meaning. Group Relations tools provide containers for play and exploration in the area of learning about authority, leadership and organization. Structure and design are the platform;

there is 'something else' and this is the way the tools are used through playing and creativity. Group Relations are deadly serious and risky; they are an endeavour that mobilizes courage as well as generosity. It is this combination that makes conferences potentially a unique experience to which all of us dedicate ever wider parts of our lives to which we invite others to share.

Part II

Themed Conferences and Group Relations Conference methodology

In this section, Ilana Litvin and Gabi Bonwitt present a paper about a conference on the very dramatic theme of 'Sexual Abuse: Application and Adaptation of Basic Group Relations Concepts, Technique and Culture to a Specific Social Issue', a conference for 'all professions in Israeli society that deal in one capacity or another with the issue of sexual abuse'. In Ross Lazar's paper 'The "Seeon" Conference', Group Relations methodology is applied to a historical conflict between two psychoanalytical societies in Germany that can be traced to the violence and tragedy of the Nazi period. The two papers have some common features.

There is an assumption in both papers that Group Relations methodology can offer an innovative way to work with very painful and anxiety-provoking themes and contexts such as conflict and violence and that new thought can emerge from this type of work and learning.

Group Relations conferences are offered as containers where difficult social issues can be re-experienced, worked through and therefore dealt with. The conference becomes a 'contained transitional space' which allows members to get in touch with difficult feelings and emotions, often totally unconscious and denied.

In these conferences, the theme pervades and invades the culture and dynamics of staff and members. Everybody is inevitably caught up in the theme. The theme sets the 'stage' and defines the 'performance'. Some of the traditional Group Relations aspects, such as leadership and authority, are important in defining the overall boundary of the conference, for example, sponsorship, management of the conference, etc., but remain in the background or fade away.

The authors of both papers demonstrate once more how the psychoanalytic concepts of splitting, projection and projective identification of unwanted parts or bad objects, as defence mechanisms against the pain of trauma and violence, are important for the understanding of inter-organizational and societal phenomena. They suggest also that awareness of these mechanisms can be helpful also in overcoming institutional impasses and in promoting new forms of freedom.

In terms of the application of Group Relations methodology, Ross Lazar emphasizes the value of the conference as a 'temporary learning organization' – how members can benefit from it as an important learning tool or from the 'microcosmic nature the laboratory setting' which 'allows for an alive and experiential interchange of emotional cognitive currents . . .'. In contrast, Ilana Litvin and Gabi Bonwitt argue that the conference is part of an 'ongoing learning forum that peaks with every additional working conference'. Use of the idea of the 'temporary learning organization' is a milestone of Group Relations conferences, but reading the two papers makes us reflect on the way the concept and method of the 'temporary learning organization' can be applied to different conferences with different tasks. In certain circumstances, the 'temporary learning organization' is enough for exploring the theme; in others, the complexity of the theme seems to require a deeper understanding which cannot be carried out only in one conference and an ongoing way of addressing it is necessary.

It should be noted that these two papers on themed conferences, which deal with the consequences of trauma and violence, are from Germany and Israel, two countries that are so directly affected and deeply bound by history.

CHAPTER THREE

Sexual abuse

Application and adaptation of basic Group
Relations concepts, technique and culture to
a specific social issue

Ilana Litvin and Gabi Bonwitt

S exual abuse, the unholiest of unholies, exists everywhere,
even in the Holy Land; let not stereotypical associations blind
us to hidden universal undercurrents. In the land of the Holy
Scripture, among the people of the Book, as anywhere else in the
human world, the unconscious obeys no moral laws, disregards
taboos, and threatens to undermine the foundations of social order.
No society escapes the ubiquitous tyranny of unconscious processes;
no society can afford to ignore or deny them.

Making sexual abuse, an arch taboo-breaking social behaviour,
the subject of OFEK's first purely socially-oriented, self-conceived
working conference may be regarded as a powerful organizational
developmental statement. Our aim in writing this paper is twofold:

1. We try to follow the conception and slow evolution of the conference on Sexual Abuse, examining it as an attempt to apply Group
   Relations' concepts, technique and culture, traditionally used in
   dealing with the issues of Authority and Leadership, to a specific
   social issue; we also point out areas in which we choose to break
   with tradition, introduce variations or changes and innovate. As
   we do so, we also demonstrate how the dynamics that develop

while dealing with the subject matter of the conference, affect our decisions, and how the process of introspection and reflection helps change some decisions, while confirming others.

2. We attempt to explore the process of creating this specific conference as an expression (both real and metaphoric) of a developmental phase in the life of our organization, a phase which also redefines its relationship to its parent organization, the Tavistock Institute's Group Relations Programme.

We start with history, briefly tracing its course, in an attempt to understand the conference's evolution. About three years ago, Esti Neeman was invited by the OFEK committee for internal learning and enrichment to lecture on the subject of Sexual Violence. The first lecture, which was followed by heated and emotionally laden discussions, led to two more evenings during which the subject was studied further. These three evenings were exceptionally well attended, an indication, we hypothesized, not only of the great interest in the subject of sexual violence, but also of its acute relevance to Israeli society in general, and its as yet unclear significance to our organization in particular. It is worth mentioning that though the number of participants wavered very little over the three evenings, the ratio of men to women changed dramatically; from eleven men and nine women in the first meeting, it shifted to three men and seventeen women in the third. The men, we assumed, felt uncomfortable, possibly attacked, possibly guilty, and tip-toed out of the added sessions, whereas the women felt a growing need to broach the subject, and were greatly relieved to be able to tackle the numerous issues it raised.

Several months later, Avi Nutkevich suggested to Esti Neeman and me (IL) that we design a working conference on the subject of sexual abuse. It was the first official venturing of OFEK into the realm of relevant social issues. Avi offered to provide ongoing supervision.

The creation of the one and a half day conference turned out to be exceptionally arduous. Our anxiety focused around the brevity of time. We were worried that one and a half days, a time frame consciously imposed upon us by economic constraints, were not enough to allow for the exploration of inner processes. We were concerned that the discourse would remain defensively rational and informative, and would not facilitate the emergence of the repressed.

Our anxiety was best exemplified by our decision to start the conference with a film, documentary or feature, that would, we hoped, reduce resistance, and help members immerse more easily in the subject of sexual abuse. We watched numerous movies, were progressively more overwhelmed by the subject, and felt less and less competent in helping others study it. Our attention was on the content, not on methods of exploring it.

Avi, whose supervision was especially gentle and 'light handed', suggested we design an inter-group event, but that we rejected, arguing that the time at our disposal was too short, and that it was too grandiose an enterprise for a first conference in which there were numerous unknown factors, the number and composition of the membership not the least of them. Our reasoning had little to do with the rationale for an inter-group event in a conference on sexual abuse; we were definitely led by our insecurity, but Avi humoured us. We resorted to the seemingly less complex, more familiar units; after the aforementioned film we would have two kinds of small study/discussion groups, intermediate plenary, review and application groups (RAGs) and a closing plenary.

When the design was ready, Esti and I asked Rina Bar-Lev Elieli to direct the conference. We did so without consulting Avi and without for a moment wondering about our authorization to choose a director, or to independently move from the planning stage to implementation. We took the mandate to stretch from inception to the actual carrying out of the complete product. We were clear about wanting a woman in the director's position. Rina, we thought, was 'maternally benevolent' and thus fit for the job. Somewhat reluctantly, she acceded to our request. We had inadvertently pushed the man out. We started acting like free agents rather than as emissaries of our organization. The solidarity among women tightened and soon took priority over our organizational loyalty. Avi, whose supervision had been an accompaniment rather than a diktat, who had left us wide room for independent thought, who had suggested rather than decreed various formats, had suddenly been 'forgotten', excluded, and become a representative of the coercive male. It can be posited that Avi himself had also been caught in the developing split, had been overly cautious rather than naturally gentle, and had unconsciously shrunk himself lest his power be interpreted as coercion. The rift (split) between men and women, which had been demonstrated in the three OFEK evenings, now gained further evidence. Avi, Esti, and myself colluded in it. Before we asked for, and were granted authorization from the board of OFEK, Rina and ourselves were busy choosing the men for the staff, expressly looking for 'non-perverse' male partners. We were clearly already steeped in the dynamics of sexual abuse, acting under the basic assumption of fight-flight, casting women as safe, and men as suspect, huddling in a same sex group, and minimizing risk by looking for docile, tameable male partners. Our identification with victimized women was unconsciously leading us to exclude virile masculinity. We were castrating our potential partners, inadvertently flipping from feeling victimized to becoming perpetrators. But at that point none of this dynamic was consciously present. We were blissfully ignorant of latent meaning; we were rather non-reflective; we were doers; we intently focused on carrying out the project we had been authorized to prepare.

It is important to mention that concomitant with that work on the conference, OFEK was going through the procedure of changing from a non-profit association, (a rather more modest contractual format), to a society for the benefit of the public. In this context, the selection of the specific social issue, (out of numerous highly relevant social issues our society at large had been struggling with), an issue that dealt with the breakdown of the family and of society was not accidental; it understandably took root, and in turn triggered the surfacing of repressed fears and conflicts. Changing OFEK's legal status, which seemed at first a benign development launched for bureaucratically financial reasons, turned out to have far-reaching ramifications. The organization was now overtly facing issues such as (1) the relationship between generations – parental figures struggling to retain, or mourning the loss of what the 'young' or newly arrived were ready to relinquish; (2) changing hierarchies – redefining relationships and working through relatedness with patrons and founders; (3) opening to the 'world' – negotiating or renegotiating relations with sibling-organizations in other countries; (4) moving from more autocratic modes of functioning to increasingly more democratic methods – having elections rather than nominating candidates for the board; allowing more independent initiatives to develop as offshoots or satellites, rather than board-initiated and controlled projects. It was, no doubt, a major organizational developmental milestone.

Design of the conference and the work of the staff

The conference in planning/in the mind underwent a dramatic change when after receiving the board's authorization, the full staff, three women and three men, started working.

It was clear from the start that we were working within the Group Relations tradition. Boundaries of time and territory, role, primary task and of course Basic Assumptions, Bion's and later additions, were very much the binding principles of our work. These concepts guided both the work of the staff, and the staff's reworking of the design of the conference. It was clear that adhering to those principles would allow for regression in the service of the ego, and would form the foundation for the contained examination of conscious and unconscious individual and group processes.

Still, though the theoretical and practical traditions were very much our guidelines, it was from within their clearly defined context that we could deviate, improvise, introduce changes, and create content-appropriate derivatives. Some of the major variations were:

1. The conference has not been perceived as a temporary organization, but as an ongoing learning forum that peaks with every additional working conference

The staff, which has so far remained unchanged, has met for seven times, pre-conference and post-conference, each meeting lasting three to four hours. The meetings formed a continuum, and contributed to staff cohesion. Each meeting had a pre-planned agenda, the issues on it depending to some extent on the proximity of the meeting to the actual conference; staff dynamics were always dealt with, and usually rendered material valuable for the understanding of the issues at hand, and therefore crucial for decision-making.

The 'on-going' organization as we identify it now, comprises seven members of staff, and a substantial body of accrued experience, concerning structural and conceptual material that forms the infra-structure for actual manifestations of specific conferences on the subject of Sexual Abuse in the Family and in Society.

So far we have had only one conference (the second one), and are now getting ready for the third, which will hopefully take place in December. It is of special interest that the first, carefully designed and planned, dated and heavily advertised conference did not materialize. Something was missing. We hypothesized that our first conference was a dress rehearsal. We were enthusiastic, but too wary and insecure to be fully committed. Somewhere we stalled for more time. There was more work to be done. This leads us directly to a crucial incident in the life of our 'on-going' organization that signified progress, and probably gave us the extra push we needed.

2. The election of the director started off as a nomination based on personal predilections, and moved, through various vicissitudes, to a democratic process that allowed for leadership to emerge, and be unanimously voted for

We nominated Rina Bar-Lev Elieli as our director, feeling fully authorized, consulting nobody, and presenting our choice as a fait accompli to the men we invited to join the staff. Under Rina's direct-orship staff coalesced and became a group strongly identified with the project. But, we hypothesize that the imbalance between women and men was not sufficiently dealt with. The history of the initial pacts and loyalties continued brewing underneath, and had to be exposed and further resolved in order for the process to move on and mature. It was Rina's resignation, in the staff meeting after the first conference did not take off, and Larry Gould's participation in, and contribution to that very meeting that paved the road for a shift in balance, and allowed freer manoeuvring within the staff. It was the organizational senior, experienced, 'parental' figures, ('mother' and 'father' who in a different context, in the same organization, had created and directed a successful program/run a functional 'fam-ily'), who by stepping aside and supporting the entire 'junior' staff, men and women alike, facilitated the beginning of a democratic and more gender-balanced process. The stage was now set for any member of staff to present his/her candidacy for director of the conference. All three women had declined taking on that role, thus opening the way for a man to assume it. This was indeed a shift in balance!

Gabi Bonwitt stepped forward, and was unanimously elected. The conference designed by women, and somewhat self righteously possessed by them, was now being more democratically shared with men. The balance between the sexes was beginning to be restored, and thus probably started removing the last obstacle that prevented the conference from materializing; this was indeed a vital step towards an honest exploration of the subject of Sexual Abuse in the Family and in Society.

3. The third variation, or deviation from traditional conference lore was the staff's attitude to the design as it was initially presented

Major changes in design resulted from circumstances, and from the staff's work as a group, and occurred at various junctions in the group work process. We give two examples. (a) In the original design, the first two small study groups were presented as three containers defined by gender. 'Men', 'Women', 'Mixed' were the labels given to these groups, and members of both sexes were free to choose which group to join and work in. As the closing date for registration approached, it became clear that we would have a majority of women (19), and a very small minority of men (2). It was then suggested and agreed that the division would shift from the membership to the consultancy, namely, that pairs of consultants, two men, two women, and a man and a woman, would each offer consultation in one of the three designated territories. It is here important to mention yet another variation. Except for the RAG groups, all small groups were consulted in tandem. We varied our consulting pairs, working in mixed pairs in the second set of small groups, but the principle remained the same. (b) The issue of the film accompanied our work throughout, and left us continuously uneasy. We just could not find the 'right' film. Whichever film we watched seemed biased in one way or another. Documentaries were too personal or too graphic; feature films were too remote or too horrid. We all watched all of them; we were either deep under their spell, or removed and assuming a movie critic's position. We were all uncomfortable. It was in the last staff meeting before the conference that it was suggested, and immediately enthusiastically accepted, that the film be replaced by a session of social dreaming. The members' and the staff's 'personal films', the pre-conference unconscious scenarios that were allowed to surface into consciousness, would be the material that formed the basis of our work. We were ready to take the leap; our anxiety subsided enough to relinquish our quasi-transitional object (which had served us extremely well), and trust our psyches. But we did not relinquish film-watching altogether; we made it optional. We arranged two territories with videos and an assortment of documentary and feature movies, and suggested it as an after-hours activity. Not surprisingly, a large number of members watched a film, and it was in the second session of social dreaming, at the opening of the second day, that emotional rather than intellectual reactions to the movies were intertwined with dream material and their associations.

4. Redefining the primary task, or adjusting traditional technique guidelines to the conference at hand, is clearly a major challenge of 'applied' Group Relations practice

Soon after our first very small RAG group, which was the closing unit of the first day, it became clear that under the circumstances, (the intense emotions aroused by the issue of sexual abuse, the small size of the group, the single consultant, the brevity of the conference as a whole, there being only two such group meetings), the RAG groups became the opportunity for a more intimate encounter, and were indeed generally used to further process some of the more urgent unfinished business of the work done during the day. Members were able to review their experience, to ponder the roles they had assumed during the first day of the conference, but they had a much harder time applying what they had learned to their life outside. Even the more experienced among them were still struggling with the learning methods and with the intensity of the experience to be able to deal with application.

5. Discussing behaviour in role, the staff agreed that since the conference tapped highly anxiety provoking issues, and since it lasted for only a day and a half, consultation would be more 'user friendly', namely staff would be more accessible to members

Here we were dealing with questions of transference, its development, its intensity, and the opportunity for its productive, even if only very partial working through, and very partial resolution. The subject matter of the conference, we hypothesized, might, in some cases, induce a powerful, positive or negative, parental, erotic transference. That in itself, one could argue, would not be exceptional. Similar phenomena occurred in conferences on Authority and Leadership, where there was more time to rework the issues. In this conference, time was short, the range of activities limited, and acquaintances brief and superficial. We felt we were dealing with explosive material that had to be handled carefully. What proportion of our caution was the staff's wariness, its anxiety over doing pioneering work in an area riddled with pain and secrecy and which part was indeed reality based, was hard to determine. To be on the safe side we assumed the harsher scenario, and dealt with the issue focusing on its basis in reality. Our assumption required drawing a fine line between accessibility and seduction, and unfailingly guarding it. Staff was not concerned with being nice or friendly to members, but rather with allaying their anxiety when it reached non-productive proportions.

The Conference that was, the Conference to be

Our dynamic observations refer to three issues: (1) location, (2) boundary between staff and membership, (3) pivotal issues.

Location

The convergence of the significance given to territory and its clear boundaries in Group Relations theory and practice, the dense meaning territory ('the territories') has assumed in the Israeli mind and existence, and the specific perversion of one's supposedly safest 'territory', home ('my home is my castle'), in the trauma of incest, has made the choice of a location for the conference a particularly fascinating and complex matter. Alongside considerations of cost, members' convenience and necessary work conditions which were obvious and conscious, there were the less or the non-conscious qualms. We wandered north and south; considered single-building hotels versus more spread out guesthouses; checked the location for its political orientation, distance from the 'green line', composition of staff, and security measures, all in an effort to feel safe. We were looking for a place that would shelter us from the dangers outside, but were of course dealing with the violence inside, and unable to feel protected from both the violent society we were part of, and the violence lodged within our individual minds.

Sexual abuse, one of the more excruciating manifestations of social violence, is on the rise in Israel. Some claim it has always been there and has, in recent years been given license to be reported, discussed and more effectively dealt with. Without assuming to tackle this question we take the liberty to say that sexual violence is a very pronounced and visible facet of the constantly escalating violence that our society suffers from. There is violence within us, and there is violence directed at us; there is a crumbling of boundaries, physical and others, and there is the erection of walls that block the horizon, isolate us and lock us in, rather than make us feel safe or sheltered. Our home is more our prison or our bunker than our castle, and that is so for citizens of all political orientations. This was the context in which we were seeking a good enough conference location. We finally decided upon the Holy Land Hotel, a once very elegant and very popular hotel in West Jerusalem, whose attraction, aside from its pool, gardens and magnificent view, had been a miniature model of the Second Temple, a symbol of Israel's magnificent past, and of its present right to the Holy Land. The hotel turned out to be more sadly run down than we had expected; still, conditions were good enough, especially thanks to the excellent service, generous and prompt, given to us by its mostly Israeli Arab staff. The staff provided us with the physical container that held the emotional one, and 'handled' us with the care and consideration that were the necessary correlate to our 'holding'. The 'location', in its physical sense, very much reflected the complexity, paradoxes, sadness and dangers our society faces on a daily basis. It was an apt place for our conference on the subject of sexual violence. Maybe our society did have better, more civil, more tolerant, more idealistic, more naïve, better kept and less violent times!? Maybe . . .

The boundary between the staff and the membership

As was said earlier, there were 21 members, nineteen women and two men. Registration was fickle. First it was slow, and then there were more than the usual number of inquiries, enrolments, cancellations, requests for full stipends etc. Some of this, we thought, reflected the dire economic situation in Israel, some the enormous interest, curiosity, ambivalence and fear associated with the subject of the conference, and with the method of studying it.

Our marketing targeted professionals rather than victims, (some professionals are, of course, also victims), but not specifically mental health professionals; our wish was to reach members of all the professions in Israeli society that deal, in one capacity or another, with the issue of sexual abuse. We hoped the membership would include police officers, lawyers, journalists, educators, physicians, nurses, etc. They, we thought, were less familiar with our professional tools and methods, and we feared we would fail to reach them. Consequently, we decided to assume a more 'user friendly' approach. Our handling the boundary between participant members and staff members was determined not only by the brevity of the conference, and the highly anxiety provoking issues it tapped, but also by the wide range of the audience we hoped to reach, the culture within and around us, and the specific point in our society's social and political situation at which we introduced our work.

There was more direct contact pre-, post- and during conference between the staff and the members. Pre-conference, the entire staff was available and involved in giving information, beyond the usual involvement in marketing of conferences. Staff were individually called, sometimes several of us by the same potential member, and asked various questions; possibly we were being 'tested' to see whether we could be trusted.

Handling of staff/membership boundaries during the conference

Our ambitions about membership composition turned out to be excessive. The membership was less diverse than we had hoped; there were educators, health professionals and people in management. There was also a woman whose occupation was revolutionary within her segment of society: she was an orthodox Jewess who practiced as an advocate for women appearing before the rabbinical courts. Professionally she was a minority of one; she was the only member who came from the judicial field, and heavily learned and practiced in judicial and ethical approaches; or so we thought, such were our projections. In the social dreaming matrix she seemed to delve straight in; she seemed to be versed in the language of emotional experience. But within four hours she voiced her decision to leave; she felt 'it was not for her'; 'this kind of learning would not benefit her', and she 'had left her children at home, and there were more important things for her to be doing'. The issue was initially raised and discussed within the first round of small groups, of which she chose the one with two women consultants. Without explicitly hypothesizing about her personal motivations, about her valency, and finding it difficult to specify how the work done with her was nuanced and different, let us only say that she was not left alone; a staff member was either close by or closely involved. When she was pressured by the members to stay, the consultants' intervention referred to the significance of respecting the voice of refusal in a conference where abuse denies exactly that. She was explicitly and actively protected from being 'abused' by the conference. A staff member had a lengthy supportive conversation with her, and both helped her leave, and left the boundary temporarily open for her return. In this case, as in others, boundaries were handled with greater flexibility, but with no less firmness than is usual in 'traditional' Group Relations conferences.

The last point relevant here is the staff's post-conference contact with the members. After the conference a letter was sent out to all participants, explicitly requesting their feedback, their reactions, comments, recommendations concerning their conference experience and future conferences. Seven out of twenty-one members responded. (There are always many informal and personal reactions after conferences; Israel is tiny, and everyone knows everyone else;

still here the responses were rather elaborate, and in writing.) The letters were focused, raised issue of design (length of conference, type of units), of content, of composition of the membership, and offered critique. They were mostly complimentary, but they were definitely not effusive. Their voice was one of empowerment rather than of admiration. In sum, we hypothesize that our way of handling the relationship between the staff and the membership enhanced rather than mitigated the learning process in a conference on a subject as sensitive as ours, and with the contextual conditions specified above.

Pivotal issues

It was no surprise to any of us that there was a large majority of women. There were moments during the registration period when we feared there would be no male participants. We were greatly relieved that our serious efforts to invite men rendered two male participants. Men and women and the relationship between them were very much the core issue of the staff's preoccupation during preparations for the conference, and not surprisingly of course, a central issue throughout the conference itself.

The subject of sexual abuse is everywhere extremely polarized. Anywhere you touch upon it the rift between men and women, the split between the masculine and the feminine is immediately evident; it manifests as a polarization between perpetrator and victim, punishment and compensation, sexual abuse or violence and sexuality, perversity and normalcy, the excluded/the pariah and the enveloped/the identified with. Morally and consciously, and in the social conscience, the poles remain wide apart – one right one wrong, one unconditionally supported the other fully and virulently condemned.

We, as the staff of the conference, never tried to oppose or reject the ethical point of view, the morally and socially essential distinction between wrong doer and victim. Our intention was to offer an additional perspective, the psychological one, which would eventually complement rather than replace the socially accepted one. Our aim, by no means a modest one, was to begin integrating the split. We wanted to find the boundary, 'spread' it into a transitional space, form an expanse where exploration could take place, where talking about sexuality in all its complexity ('perversity' included), would be permitted. We wanted to explore the hidden nooks where perpetrator and protector of victims cohabited, where one's projections were one's owned wishes.

Throughout our work there were numerous examples of learning in this deepest sense, instances where via associations the 'polymorphous perverse' was tapped, and courageously dealt with rather than repressed or otherwise defended against. In one of the small groups a participant member described her excitation, when as a child she would repeatedly be accosted with the penis of an exhibitionist, which reminded her of a fireman's water pipe. She giggled as she retrieved the memory, realizing that it was a confusing experience, part offensive part attractive, part frightening part titillating or even soothing, (he would put out the fire).

On another occasion, during the second session of social dreaming, a member who had on the previous evening seen 'War Zone', Tim Roth's excellent feature film on incest, was able to talk about her sexual arousal while watching the father subject his daughter to anal sex. She felt ashamed at finding herself excited by what she knew she socially clearly condemned, yet she was able to share it with the entire membership and staff, and was responded to with further associations rather than with moral condemnation.

Hers was the voice of integration; she owned perversity, acknowledged its presence in inner life, and from within this newly 'thought known' could proceed working towards fuller integration of split off parts, towards reparation. She seemed to be able to do it within herself, but her voice, and the way it reverberated throughout the membership also suggested that it was being done in the conference as a whole.

We regard our experience as further evidence that the Group Relations model, its theory and technique, is applicable to working with social issues that surface from the depth of society's unconscious, and seem to suddenly become the focus of public attention for reasons not immediately apparent.

CHAPTER FOUR

The 'Seeon' Conference

Group Relations as applied to a historical conflict between two professional groups. An exercise in experiencing, understanding and dealing with inter-group and institutional conflict

Ross A. Lazar

A Chassidic Aforethought

There is the Thought, the Word and the Deed ... for the man who gets all three straight within himself, for him all things will turn towards the Good.

With this short quote, taken from his wonderful little book *Der Weg des Menschen nach der chassidischen Lehre* (*The Way of Man according to Chassidic Teaching*), Martin Buber (1960) epitomises the source of what he believes to be the 'deepest and hardest problem of our lives', namely, 'the *true source of conflict between men*' [author's emphasis] (p. 34).

In this paper I will examine the application of the Group Relations approach in conjunction with a historically determined conflict between two psychoanalytic professional groups. Over the course of my experience in Group Relations, it has become apparent to me that many of the most significant and virulent differences between political and professional groups were differences which Freud would have attributed to 'the narcissism of small differences'. That is to say, not issues of fundamental incompatibility or difference, but rather those based on intolerance of similarity, played a major role in causing such conflicts. The relevance of this in the planning and execution of the Seeon Conference soon became evident.

Background, history and preparation for the Conference

Historically, the background of the Seeon Conference takes us back to the roots of anti-Semitism in German Christian culture (Beland, 1990), as well as to the atrocities of the Nazi regime during its twelve year reign. It takes us back to the chaos and confusion of a devastated and defeated post-war Germany and to the special fate that psychoanalysis and the psychoanalytic movement underwent, both during and immediately after the Nazi period. And it takes us into the midst of the political and economic situation of the recent past and the very present in the Federal Republic, especially in the spheres of the training of psychoanalysts and psychoanalytic psychotherapists and the delivery of, control over and payment for psychoanalytic/psychotherapeutic treatment.

Also it takes us back to Nazareth, where the first Group Relations Working Conference between German and Israeli psychoanalysts was held under the direction of Eric Miller in 1994. This conference, co-sponsored by OFEK (Organization, Person, Group, the Israel Association for the Study of Group and Organizational Processes), the IPS (Israel Psychoanalytic Society), the IAP (Israel Association of Psychotherapy) for the Israelis; and by *both* the *Deutsche Psychoanalytische Gesellschaft* (DPG – German Psychoanalytical Society) and the *Deutsche Psychoanalytische Vereinigung* (DPV – German Psychoanalytical Association) representing German psychoanalysts, took place under the auspices of the Sigmund Freud Centre for Psychoanalysis of the Hebrew University of Jerusalem and the Tavistock Institute. The reason I refer to this first Nazareth Conference as a key factor in the prehistory of the Seeon Conference derives from the experiences which particularly the German participants had there.

As the planning for the first Nazareth Conference took shape, the joint sponsoring by DPG and DPV – an event in itself unprecedented – became an additional undeniably important conference theme. The hypothesis was advanced that a historically based and extremely painful conflict would become manifest. This conflict centred on the splitting of the original German Psychoanalytic Society, founded by Karl Abraham in Berlin in 1910, into the two separate organisations, DPG and DPV, which took place as an aftermath of the Nazi period in 1949–50. One of the most painful areas concerned the fact that, following the end of World War II, only the newly-formed split-off organisation, DPV, received international recognition by the International Psychoanalytic Association, while the DPG was refused this recognition on the basis of its work no longer being truly psychoanalytic. But during the preparations for 'Nazareth' the entire complex subject of DPG-DPV relations was hardly mentioned, and certainly did not become a major focus of conference work.

Retrospectively this seemed to many German members, especially members of the executive boards of both organisations, to be an alarming signal. Evidently the threat that these issues posed was too large to even think about, never mind voice. Nevertheless, despite these anxieties, the idea that the DPG and the DPV might jointly sponsor their own Group Relations conference was born. A working conference was to be commissioned to be executed by a third party, namely MundO. MundO, derived from the German words *Menschen und Organizationen* (human beings and organisations) a charitable society, founded in 1982, had since its inception as its main purpose the organisation of Group Relations work in German-speaking Europe. The conference itself was to be held at Kloster Seeon in Bavaria in Southern Germany, and carried out under the author's direction by an international staff of experienced Group Relations professionals.

As a first step, MundO developed a proposal for the implementation of the event, including the selection of the director, the conference design (especially conceived for and tailored to the task with the help of Eric Miller), a staffing plan, an appropriate venue and a financial plan. The two delegates of the sponsoring organisations meanwhile were to do some 'market research' as to how many of their members would be interested in attending such a conference.

Even at this early stage, certain important trends indicative of the conflicts involved, immediately manifested themselves. For instance: there were dramatic differences in support for the event from each of the two organisations memberships and the different ways in which the two representatives went about canvassing their memberships for potential conference members were very noticeable. Other important differences had to do with the willingness of the respective leaders and office holders to support the conference in general, specifically by making a commitment to its taking place at all, by their readiness to attend as members; and by their willingness to take financial responsibility for any loss which the conference might generate.

As a next step, the history, themes, aims and methods, membership requirements and primary task were set out in a brochure which was then sent to all members of both organisations.

In this brochure the conference *aim* was defined as 'to facilitate exchange (dialogue) between the members of the DPG and the members of the DPV in order to better understand the consequences of the historic splitting of the psychoanalytic community in Germany on their current situation and relationships in the present'.

The primary task of the conference was defined as: 'to explore and exchange, within the boundaries of this conference, personal experiences of the various consequences (both conscious and unconscious, individual and collective) resulting from the division of the German psychoanalytic community that took place in 1949–50, in order to ascertain their effect upon and their meaning for psychoanalysts in Germany today'.

The 54 available membership places were offered 50/50 to each organisation, and in order to make the boundary somewhat more porous, the criterion for conference membership was stated as being 'as a general rule' a member in one or the other of the two organisations.

The description of the method stated that it derived from the Tavistock Group Relations model and was developed from both a psychoanalytic and a systems-analytic understanding of people-in-role in groups and organisations.

The conference dynamic itself

From the BEGINNING: 'Let's call the whole thing off!'

The first striking event took place at the beginning of the opening plenary and consisted of a statement by the eldest member that the whole issue of the split between the two psychoanalytic societies was unnecessary and in any case a bad thing. His suggestion was to merge the two societies immediately and thus do away with the entire unfortunate business! This statement in its naiveté and direct-ness caused some amusement, but, in fact, had to be taken extremely seriously. No sooner had the group assembled and the first traces of the anxieties it caused become apparent, than it managed to mobilise a member to be its 'flight' leader. Equally, such a defensive move, while eliminating the need for painful emotional conflict for the moment, would at the same time have eliminated any possibility for new understandings, any possibilities of working through the con-flicts and consequently any possible learning from the experience.

The 'Jewish question': a question for whom?

The next highly controversial and threatening theme was the impact of the forced resignation of the Jewish members of the DPG (in December, 1935) on the identity of psychoanalysts in Germany today, on their relationships with one other and with the larger world of psychoanalysis internationally. The persecution and forced emigration of Jews from Nazi Germany and especially of Jewish psychoanalysts was brought into focus by the observation that if Freud had not immigrated to England in 1939, he most likely would have been murdered in a concentration camp. Linked to this were many members' experiences of being rejected, of being snubbed, avoided, of not being taken seriously, and even of outward rejection and hatred stemming from members of the psychoanalytic world outside Germany.

In terms of the conference dynamic, this found immediate and direct transferential expression in the reactions of the members to the fact that some staff members were either of Jewish descent and upbringing themselves or had had Jewish forebears, some of whose lives were directly affected by the Nazi regime.

On understanding and misunderstanding

Valuing and devaluing; helpfulness and destructiveness; insults and prejudices

The upshot of this and all the other conflicts which quickly arose between members and staff immediately led to the membership feeling itself to be misunderstood, devalued, rejected and the subjects of devastating criticism by the staff. This, in turn, led them to react in kind, and, experiencing the staff's contributions to be bad, ill-fitting and unhelpful, to reject them. But even 'helpful', 'positive' interpretations were also misunderstood and transformed into critical, devaluating statements. These insults and injuries, this criticising and fault-finding, were not restricted to the DPG–DPV conflict alone, but was equally rampant among members *within* the boundaries of their own organisations. Thus it began to emerge that the two were involved in a massive system of splitting-and-projection, of projective identifications and their introjections, which for a long time had served to stabilise the identities of both. Given the opportunity to explore this within the relative safety of the conference setting, and to project into a new and different and separate object (i.e. into the staff and the conference institution as a whole), it slowly became possible to extract oneself somewhat from these old patterns, to view the whole process and the structures in which it took place in a new light.

Dare a German psychoanalyst consider him/herself a psychoanalyst at all?

Another of the most painful questions was raised early on by a leading member of the DPV. He put forth the hypothesis that *both* groups of German psychoanalysts – indeed one would have to assume *all*, or at least all *non-Jewish*, German psychoanalysts – suffer from what he called a 'taboo of assuming ownership' (*Aneignungstaboo*) vis-à-vis psychoanalysis itself. His hypothesis was that the unconscious guilt resulting from the expulsion and murder of their Jewish colleagues prevented psychoanalysts in Germany from legitimately inheriting the legacy of the 'Freudian-Jewish science' of psychoanalysis to this very day. Analogous to those German citizens who profited by taking over businesses, apartments and houses, goods and furniture, jewellery, money and gold, etc. from their Jewish neighbours, it could be said that German psychoanalysts, even if, by now, they have legitimately gained the 'legal' right to consider themselves proper heirs to the Freudian bequest, still actually feel themselves not entitled to its possession.

Therefore it should have come as no surprise to anyone that they would want to try to foist this feeling off on to someone else. And who might suit the role of receiver of such split-off projections better than one's closest cousins, those whose family of origin was identical with one's own, but who, through their particular fate, either chose to or were forced by circumstances to remain part of the original family constellation, while the others went off and founded a new branch? As it turned out, however, it was not just the DPG analysts who were seen to be and/or felt themselves to be insecure in their psychoanalytic identity, a fact which should have surprised no one.

Ritual battles fought in the name of the avoidance of real conflict

Instead of being able to talk to one another about the real and/or imagined similarities and differences, instead of carrying on an earnest and constructive exchange of thoughts, feeling and experiences, instead of following on from one another's contributions, and/or indeed instead of breaking out in *real* battles, many of the conference events, the plenary sessions in particular, were, to use a member's term, often characterised by 'ritual battles' as a means of defence. Obviously, it was much easier to cry the battle cries of past battles, or even those of current battles in different theatres of war, than to face off in the here-and-now.

Thus, fighting these ritual battles proved effective in keeping down or avoiding altogether anything like open conflict. The nearest any one or any group came to openly engaging with any other took place at the level of territoriality. Here, different interpretations of the 'rules and regulations' as well as the 'rights' of individuals and groups to be in, to use, occupy or even block a particular territory for use by others, led to more or less direct confrontations of various sorts. At these moments, tempers got roused and the frightening nearness of physical violence and mob rule between the parties in conflict became palpable. But, in the end the anger, disappointment and hatred got directed towards the staff, *not* towards one another. Blaming the staff for creating such unclear situations, for not expediting their clarification, and most of all for not protecting the participants from the necessity of engaging in open conflict was clearly felt to be the responsibility and therefore the fault of the staff group. But I assume that, in the end, the symbolic meaning of these clashes had become clear to all.

Crisis and resolution: The eldest member of staff and the only German-Jewish psychoanalyst takes on the role of 'Seelenklempner' for the Membership

In a newspaper review of his new book, the then Israeli Ambassador to Germany, Avi Primor, was referred to as someone who is often expected to be a *'Seelenklempner'*, a 'soul plumber' for the German people, that is, one to whom the Germans turn in order to have themselves psychically 'repaired'. At an absolutely crucial moment in the conference this very role fell to *our* Israeli staff member who was expected symbolically to fulfil exactly this task. Indeed, it had been a common fantasy right from the very beginning that the influence of the conference in general and of the MundO staff in particular, might prove 'psycho-hygienically' beneficial to the internal states of both institutions, as well as to their relationship with one another. This was voiced in the fantasy that MundO might act as a kind of 'organisational therapist' for the two psychoanalytic organisations, putting them both on the 'organisational couch' as it were.

Thus, it was only logical that the oldest, wisest and furthermore only manifestly Jewish member of staff should be expected to take on this role. It was as if he were being asked to absolve the sins of the German members, real and fantasised, present and past, as well as to take kindly to their efforts towards reparation, of which symbolically, he was to be the recipient. If he could play this role and accept these efforts, then some expiation of guilt and of guilt feelings could be assumed. If he, in the name of the staff, of international psychoanalysis and of the outside world, rejected them, then . . . well then, what? In fact, this outcome was nearly unthinkable. It seems in retrospect that

that was not even an option! For if he, if we as a staff, had rejected these reparative efforts and sentiments, the hurt and the hopelessness, the guilt and the hatred unleashed would have become quite unbearable and possibly uncontainable by the conference institution.

Since the staff had done so much work on continually trying to interpret to the members the various ways in which they were avoiding, projecting and otherwise attempting to neutralise their destructiveness, it was logical that the membership wanted and needed to hear from that same staff that all was not in vain. Interpretations around the signs of murderousness, of 'vampire-like greed' in the membership or of severe feelings of inadequacy and insecurity in their individual and collective identities as German psychoanalysts were experienced as extremely painful, sometimes as unfair or cruel, even as maddening.

Equally it was just as impossible for DPV members to grant absolution to their DPG counterparts as it was for them to *receive* such absolution for the 'sins of the Fathers' from the International Psychoanalytic Association. So who else could have served as a more appropriate authority to grant this than a German-born, internationally renowned and admired Jewish psychoanalyst of the elder generation – a man who even bore the name of God's own Law Bringer!

The end of the Conference

By the end, most participants had begun to engage themselves actively in the pursuance of the primary task of the conference, even if it took some time before they became able and willing to do so, and even if, as always, some were able to understand and accept it better than others and were, therefore, in a better position to work towards it. Common to all, however, was the need to defend against a whole range of terribly painful and upsetting insights, both at the individual and collective levels, none of which had anything to do, except in a transference sense, with the staff group itself as such. But most important of all, the inevitable necessity of recognising and continuing to mourn the traumatic and tragic, the irretrievable, irrevocable personal and collective loss to psychoanalysis as a science and as a profession, as well as to German culture and the culture at large was at least realised as unavoidable, if not personally acceptable to all.

Characterised as 'one of the most important experiences and discoveries of the conference', this was well expressed by one member when she said, 'In the end, it seemed as if the whole thing would just have to begin all over again'. She continued by saying, 'as long as we do nothing but fight one another, argue with one another and denigrate and devalue one another, as long as we continually look for, discover and fight the "bad" and the "evil" in the other professional society, we don't have to occupy ourselves with the problem of our standing in the tradition of German psychoanalysis, and, with that, with the exclusion and expulsion of our Jewish colleagues. Also, we needn't occupy ourselves with the likelihood that Freud himself, had he not been able to flee in time, would most likely have been murdered in a German concentration camp. We are saved from having to confront the question of a possible 'taboo of ownership' of the inheritance of psychoanalysis, that is, it saves us . . . and therefore *prevents* us from exercising it self-assuredly and as a matter of course, not to mention passionately and creatively.'

Another main thing which the conference did achieve was at least to *begin* a process of reflection *at the organisational and institutional level* of conflicts and the areas of controversy and disagreement, as well as those of similarity and commonality of interest, which might contribute to their ability to act co-operatively in the pursuit of common aims in future. There is much work still to be done to identify those areas of political, professional and societal work, and on developing *modi vivendi* to enable and increase tolerance and acceptance of existing and undeniably significant differences, which can neither be ignored nor minimised, but also need not be unnecessarily and damagingly exaggerated.

The main areas of conflict and their vicissitudes

Benefits and burdens of the Group Relations model

By the end of the conference more questions had been raised than answered, more problems posed than solved, more conflicts unearthed than buried. Does this mean the conference was a failure? Or that the Group Relations method, insofar as it inevitably has such an effect, creates more problems than it solves? If one has had the fortune to have benefited from the kind of new-found freedom, both of thought and of action, which this method can bring forth, both for oneself and one's organisation, such doubts are counteracted by these new and liberating experiences. But it is not our task to debate the pros and cons of the method here; instead I want to outline again the main conflicts which this undertaking presented us and to indicate briefly what happened to each of them.

Eliminating potential conflict: a special form of hatred of learning from experience

Statements to the effect that as a member of the DPV one could not expect to learn anything from the DPG (or from the DPV itself for that matter, a thought which was also voiced), seem in retrospect also to mean 'I expect to learn nothing from this conference'. In other words, they give voice to that *hatred of learning from experience* of which Bion speaks and in which we all participate. This ubiquitous dynamic seemed in Seeon to be underpinned by a basic assumption of flight – flight from the new, from the unknown, indeed flight from the truth itself. In so doing this also served as a protective shield against the kind of radical rearrangement of reality to which Bion gave the name *catastrophic change*. If nothing new is to be expected, and nothing to be learned, then nothing need change at all!

The historical conflicts

It seemed that a great deal of important, albeit painful, work got done at the level of consciousness-raising and the establishing of relatedness *vis-à-vis* the historical relations of the two societies. It did seem possible to join in common acknowledgement of the feelings of collective guilt, shame and genuine sorrow about the fate of Jewish colleagues in the 1930s, of the damaging effect which the events of the Nazi period have had on psychoanalysis in Germany right up to the present day and of the common past of *all* German psycho-analysts, regardless of which professional society they happen to belong to today. But here problems begin again. For it seems that certain basic conflicts surrounding tradition and ideology, standards of training and standards of work proved to be as hot and controversial as ever, and as equally irresolvable as they were before. Still, the conference was able to provide a new kind of forum for their acknowledgement and exploration, which, at the institutional level, had not existed before.

Perhaps the most difficult conflict and the one which provides the connecting link from the past to the present, is the accusation that the DPG and its members subscribed to and are still infiltrated with and influenced by beliefs, ideas and procedures which are seen and felt to be profoundly *anti-psychoanalytic*. This feeling has to do with the actual or imagined co-operation of the generation of the 'fathers' with M. Goering and the Nazi-run 'German Institute' in Berlin, and with a presumed ongoing allegiance to ideas and techniques promulgated by one of its most prominent members, Harald Schulz-Hencke. For undoubtedly, Schulz-Hencke had had the most profound formative influence on the whole post-war generation of teachers and training analysts of anyone from the 'old' DPG. Furthermore, the accusation of being *anti-psychoanalytic* carries with it an implied accusation of latent anti-Semitism. A latent feeling that DPG members are, purely by virtue of their organisational affiliation, somehow tainted, that they are almost felt to be 'pariahs' or to be the illegitimate offspring of 'badly baptised' parents seemed to run as an undercurrent throughout all the interchanges between the two societies.

The other side of that conflict takes the form of accusation that the members of the DPV consider themselves to be the 'clean ones', the 'holy ones', the 'chosen people', and that, accordingly, they acted in an arrogant, intolerant, self-righteous and snobbish manner. This was understood for the most part to be a defensive stance, designed to protect DPV members from 'contamination' by the above-mentioned 'uncleanness'. Whereas it certainly was significant that this phenomenon could be named and explored, I have little evidence that anything much happened during the conference to alter these feelings and fantasies *at the institutional level*.

The current conflicts

Moving on to the areas of current conflict, again there was little to make one think that any major changes in the relationships of the two societies had occurred, other than that they were in better contact with one another. Presumably, as some of these conflicts, especially those to do with the negotiations with the health insurance authorities, are still so fresh, and in part still unresolved, it is impossible to imagine that any realistic solutions might have been sought and found at the moment. But again, the opportunities which the conference offered, both for the exploration of similarities and differences, for the comparison of experiences and the testing of fantasy against fact, rather than relying on guesswork and projection, cannot prove other than helpful in the search for truth.

Conclusion

In the end one finds oneself asking questions like: Taken altogether then, what was this undertaking all about? What was it in terms of what it was meant to be? To be quite fair, one must admit that for some it did nothing at all; for others it apparently only made things worse; and for some it was quite interesting, perhaps, but in the end probably not really worth the time, effort and money involved in participating.

But obviously, for others it becomes quite a significant and potent experience, one full of new possibilities, feelings, thoughts and insights into the nature of individuals, groups and organisations, and one with considerable potential for change, even for 'catastrophic change' at all these levels. The microcosmic nature of the laboratory setting which the formation of a temporary conference institution creates, allows for an alive and lively experiential interchange of the emotional and cognitive currents and movements contained within an organisation and its members, for their recognition and for their study. In the case of issues of conflict, whatever their source, they can and should be able to be 'contained' within the conference institution, scrutinised, pondered over and interpreted. And from that process should emerge something new: new feelings, new thoughts, a new insight into the dynamics and relationships involved.

In this sense the Group Relations approach is the pendant at the group and institutional level to the process which Buber enjoins us to engage in at the individual level. By its very nature, it never has nor will solve one single human conflict. It neither claims for itself, nor does it subscribe to the belief that conflicts can be 'resolved' in the sense described above. However, by providing the means, i.e., the setting and the tools for experiencing the reality of relationships, for gaining insight into them, and therefore increasing the possibilities, and hence the likelihood for changes in human systems, it provides a unique and valuable service, which no other comparable method can equal. It provides no guarantee that anyone or any group might find its way from the paranoid-schizoid to the depressive position, not even for one moment. Equally, it does not and cannot provide any security whatsoever that work group activity will preside over basic assumption activity. Whether this, in the end, will lead us any closer to the 'Good' or not, as Buber suggests, I do not know. But it does seem to me to be a plausible thought, and until proven otherwise, well worth trying.

Postscript: Conference follow-up

The first official working meeting of the two societies

In June, 1997, one year after the conference took place, the current chairmen of the two societies invited a small group of representatives from each organisation to Frankfurt am Main to participate in the first *official* working conference ever to be held between the DPG and the DPV as such. In a report of that meeting in the DPV Information Bulletin of October 1997, an executive board member of the DPV and ex-participant of the Seeon Conference wrote that this conference 'could in a certain sense be understood to be a continuation of the Seeon Conference, albeit in a completely different form and with a different goal.' (Trimborn, 1997). The atmosphere is reported to have been both 'open and spontaneous' and to have been, on the whole, 'concrete in a satisfying way.' At the same time, 'a continuation of the dialogue will continue to show up the differences [between the two organisations] with even greater clarity.' Still, all concerned were said to be looking forward to the next meeting with excitement and interest. Is this new attempt at rapprochement to be understood as a function, perhaps even a direct result of the Seeon Conference? Would it have ever occurred in this way if there hadn't been a Seeon Conference, or would it have happened anyway?

Part III

The application of Group Relations Conferences methodology to professional roles

This section brings together ideas around the application of Group Relations conference work and professional roles.

Karen Izod uses Group Relations thinking that encourages active enquiry and experimental engagement in case examples that show how both individuals and organisations grapple with managing the social trend and organisational imperative for individuals to take ownership of their careers. She also suggests how managing a career portfolio requires both an engagement with and a distancing from one's own work, a capacity to use the security structures of the organisation to allow greater mobility, to foster interdependence, and to examine ways in which core business, structures and processes can influence its position on a dependency-to-autonomy continuum. Izod proposes a return to the concept of the socio-technical system, a system of work which allows for the social and emotional needs of the worker to be aligned along with industry and sector technology. Individuals need to be self-regulating and self-organising; consequently, a socio-technical balance requires a shift away from independence or autonomy to a more mutually derived interdependence.

Carl Mack's paper argues that an ecological approach can be a useful and successful model for conceptualising the achievement gap exhibited by black students, but it needs to be dynamically shaped to include the centrality of groups and the unconscious processes that will occur during any transformative effort. He suggests that when transformation reaches the stage in which research is necessary to clarify issues of the students and their families, then a concomitant level of 'action research' should be used to clarify the unconscious processes that *will* take place at the individual, group and organisational levels. Mack is clear that working on the unconscious is not a panacea, and that changes in US public school organisational structures and processes must occur in order to be effective in improving education for all children in general and specifically for black students. Strong feelings will arise when organisational dynamics of dependency emerge; therefore implementation of research-based innovations should recognise this as part of a deep process that gives children and adults (parents, guardians, teachers and administrators) the opportunity and support to work through the anxiety and conflict that accompanies any transformation in structure, purpose or process. To change educational systems that have perpetuated injustice over a long time requires much 'internal' organisational work.

Siv Boalt Boëthius uses her role as visiting professor consultant to challenge the general assumptions in working life that resources of staff, leadership, economy, technical equipment etc. will automatically be used constructively; that there will inevitably be capacity for developing adequate structures, and that boundaries around the work will naturally be containing. She presents a case where external and internal threats and conflicts took over the consultation work. In order for her work to continue, it was necessary to cope with and integrate the basic assumptions of a university culture. At a university clinic, which had research, training and treatment functions, she found that the different types of work evoked different kinds of basic assumptions, which tended to clash. She describes how she found managing her consultant role reflected in the conflict of the university clinic's primary tasks – of the university to provide conditions for academic education and research where the underlying basic assumption is fight-flight, and the psychotherapy clinic where the underlying basic assumption is characterised by dependency.

CHAPTER FIVE

Mutuality and interdependence

Applications of Group Relations perspectives to issues of career ownership and development

Karen Izod

Thinking about career development often evokes an idea of change from one professional identity to another, or from one organisation to another, where there is hope for a better fit. But in this knowledge economy a newer notion of career is emerging. It relates not so much to what an identity or a workplace can offer, as to how and where experience and skills can be accumulated over time, and how and where these can adjust to organisational need and market trends. Career development therefore embraces both an idea of movement *between* identities and organisations, and movement or expansion *within* identities and organisations.

The concept of 'career ownership' is currently being used to describe a shift away from the organisation as a provider of traditional and usually hierarchical career progression, to one of individuals as seekers of their own career opportunities (Holbeche, 2000). It suggests a changing relatedness between the individual and the organisation, or the individual and their work-place identity, where career choice and employment status is subject to flux and change. Career trajectories are increasingly less bound by organisational structures and professional pathways, and more open to what the individual and the organisation require and can create in the moment.

I will be exploring some of my thinking about the interplay between individual and organisation which is brought into being through this notion of career ownership in the context of the learning that occurs in Group Relations conference work. The focus will be upon the nature of career ownership as it is encountered in large organisations, where intra-organisational and multiple system dynamics are at play.

I see this presentation as being relevant for consultants working out of an applied systems-psychodynamic perspective, as well as for HR professionals engaged in thinking about supporting career development initiatives.

A transitional framework: conference work to organisational life

To use Group Relations perspectives in my work as an organisational consultant involves firstly relating to a core theoretical underpinning which draws upon multiple psychoanalytic and organisational theories, and brings into play constructs as to what organisation is, i.e. organisation as collage, (Hatch, 1997) organisation as cultures (Morgan, 1986). Over-layering this might be current thoughts about roles, boundaries, tasks and the nature of authority (Gertler & Izod, 2004) and how these concepts help me in asking questions, and attempting to diagnose and intervene in organisational life.

Adding conference experience to these theoretical perspectives, I am looking at what especially it is that happens, is felt, gets articulated, and may ultimately be learned from, that makes it possible to step from participation in an experiential learning event to engaging in lived organisational and consulting dilemmas.

In doing so, the following formulations create something of a transitional framework for application:

> How conference life for participants and staff members alike, can provide fertile ground to work in a spirit of enquiry – exploring, encountering and thereby contributing to an organisation in the making, together with a realisation of the imperative for action –

intervening in and shaping that organisation's capacities and resistances to development and change.

How conference work can provide an illumination of organisational cultures, both as they are experienced in the mind of
individuals and in its emergent structures and practices.

Put together, to apply Group Relations perspectives to one's own
organisational activities, might be to foster approaches to work
which promote active enquiry and experimental engagement in the
face of preferred and persistent ways of doing things.

These approaches are essentially to do with establishing modes of
behaviour between individuals and organisations. They specifically
challenge issues of dependency and autonomy. As I shall go on to
explore with the theme of career ownership, they raise the concept
of inter-dependence and mutuality – what it means to individuals
and their internal cultures, and to organisations and their practices,
when responsibilities for managing careers take on a different
character.

Furthering application: research orientation

I have outlined both a theoretical underpinning and transitional
framework to the question of application, but doing so leaves out
something less definable, which is to do with the rich and powerful
texture of conference experience. Something about the extra-
ordinary experiences that participants and staff alike are thrown
into, the struggle to manage one's senses and emotions in the presence of the unfamiliar, and the struggle to access one's cognitive
resources to be able to think and not just fall back on repeating
patterns of behaviour.

With greater exposure to these encounters, in becoming more
knowledgeable participants and staff members, then so these
experiences of being unearthed and thrown about can become more
familiar, but rarely comfortable. Yet as an organisational consultant,
I face a challenge not only in recognising when this is happening in
conference work, when to some extent I have this in mind and
am in role to work with it, but in noticing when client systems are

encountering this phenomenon – when they themselves are uprooted, experiencing something for the first time, and likely encountering resonance with much earlier emotions and constructions. And, inevitably, when I also am in that upheaval, having to manage these things for myself, in structures and roles which usually do not afford a comparable containment to conference structures and roles.

And so I would say that a significant application of conference work involves working from a position in which it is possible to identify and retain awareness of when client systems are in this kind of turbulence, and together with the range of theoretical orientations available, to use the experience of being in there to inform my thinking and range of interventions available. In particular, in my consulting practice, I see this duality of experience and theory as yielding data which can be used diagnostically, in shaping the kind of questions I feel I need to ask, or in laying the ground for dialogue – placing these sets of skills in an action research mode, rather than something which derives from an interpretative, educative or therapeutic mode.

Furthering application: organisational culture

I have mentioned how conference work can provide an illumination of organisational culture, both as it is experienced in the mind of individuals and in its emergent structures and practices. My suggestion is that when a conference works from a psychoanalytic perspective, what it does is to illuminate and help us question the nature of organisational culture, as an array of images which may or may not be coherent amongst individuals. Smircich (1983) in her paper on concepts of culture and organisational analysis speaks of the psychoanalytic understanding of culture as being seen in the unconscious infra-structures that are created and revealed in organisational culture; that culture is an internal as well as an external variable.

Similarly, when a conference works from an organisational theory or systems perspective, then what it can do is illuminate the contextual issues or the external culture that is impinging. What are we seeing that is happening in society or the immediate organisational environment, in terms of the location of power, the need for corporate responsibility, the nature of participation in decision-making and so on?

And conference work in general tries to make the connections between these internally created and externally experienced constructions of organisation.

Many of the changes in working structures and practices, which underpin organisational cultures, are created in response to environmental demands, and usually economic constraint. They are often followed by a human resource rationale, or indeed by a postmodern epistemology to suggest that these practices are part and parcel of contemporary life. Some of the features of current working life can make an appearance in this way; hot-desking, flexible working, coaching and mentoring, can all be seen as organisations' attempts to find innovative solutions to financial constraint and survival, often by placing greater demands on the individual, and maintaining the existing power balance. How we experience these initiatives will depend on our capacities to find something good in them for ourselves, and this in turn is often influenced by our age, and how we have internalised or created our own images of work and the workplace. Cynicism can prevail on the one hand, a feeling that there is no choice and one's only option is to be compliant or leave (dependent or autonomous), whilst a more positive seeing of opportunity can emerge on the other, and pleasure had at increased opportunity (interdependence).

Application in practice: an educational intervention

To give an example of these two elements: At a personal and professional development programme I worked on for women, I introduced a brief event with the purpose of illuminating the dynamics and processes involved in networking. Rather like an inter-group event, the participants had half an hour to identify between themselves networks that they would like to form (which had the potential to carry on after the workshop) in which they could discuss topics of professional interest between them. A further hour was available for the networking groups to work together, and for individuals to move or re-form. As it happened, after some initial enquiry about boundaries, individuals formed groups with those that they were standing near, with little movement around the room to enquire about, or contribute to the choices being generated. Conversations were interesting but lacked vitality, and no further movements occurred.

What could be learned from this? This was not a Group Relations event, and we were not working in interpretative mode. Instead there was an opportunity for all of us to review what happened in terms of organisational and individual process. Most participants identified that regardless of what the topic might be, or what they hoped to gain for their individual development, their choices were founded on a need to belong and to not become isolated. To choose between individuals with a view to furthering one's own learning, and with the possibility of furthering one's own position seemed an impossibility, even though this had been agreed as a task they were willing to collaborate upon.

The event provided an opportunity to generate ideas and data about the interplay between the individual, the task, and the nature of the organisation, and to stimulate further questions. This was an intense temporary learning organisation of women which had been formed for several days generating a culture where the need to belong and to minimise differentiation assumed priority over a more explorative and self-determining task. It was also not that dissimilar to many of the back-home working environments that the participants came from.

I give this example as a way of illustrating a more research-oriented application in an educational setting, which links to internal and external cultures being created, but also as a way of demonstrating the kind of dilemmas that people face in networking, which is a central element in managing one's own career.

Introducing career ownership

Practices and behaviours associated with career ownership can occupy a space between organisational cultures as they are experienced in the internal type 'infra-structures' that are created and ways of doing things that respond to contextual, societal demand.

I have suggested how career ownership is a term given to the practice of taking responsibility for one's own career trajectory. It is both an economic measure, as companies can no longer support hierarchical structures and practices which provide a traditional career path, and a social or ideological measure, as individuals increasingly want to create their own futures, and find flexible ways of doing so. Career ownership requires a commitment to self-directed learning and development, along with a capacity to identify and seek out opportunities to position one's self well for the next move. Career progression is seen no longer as linear, but as encompassing multiple positions and routes. In effect, individuals often need to find ways of moving from a dependent set of behaviours such as those inherent in bureaucracies and hierarchies, to behaviours which are much more autonomous and self-organising, and undertake the kind of exploratory, self-authorising movement around organisational structures which individuals are able to explore in conference work.

Within this framework, organisations are required to work in partnership with their staff. Hall and Moss (1998), quoted in a study of career paths undertaken by Holbeche (2000), comment that the most effective organisations will not attempt to manage careers as in the past, but will provide opportunities for continuing learning. They will shift from being a direct career provider to being an enabler or broker of career paths, which may also include the reality that better opportunities might exist elsewhere. Hence organisations take up this enabling role, by offering a range of professional development interventions, career development workshops, secondments into other parts of the organisation, mentoring and so on.

Introducing inter-dependence

My belief is, however, that partnerships between individuals and organisations, which require individuals to take up the more exploratory and self-authorising roles that I have described, can only be possible, given an organisational culture that will encourage and sustain behaviours of a more autonomous kind, and that ultimately one is looking for a mutuality or interdependency between the individual and the organisation if retention of a coherent workforce is to be possible.

Group Relations work draws much upon Miller's (1993) ideas, and his continuum of development from dependency to autonomy. But here, I would like to think more about a middle position, which acknowledges inter-dependence or the mature and mutual dependence of one system upon another, in which both parts need to acknowledge the need of one for the other, without being overly reliant and sustained on the one hand, or overly separate and disengaged on the other.

Inter-dependence, between organisation and worker, will inevitably mean a greater taking up of power on behalf of the individual, and a willingness to give up power on the part of the organisation, as with other programmes of employee empowerment. Without organisation as provider of career paths, individual behaviour which is too dependent will generally result in atrophy and lack of progress, whereas behaviour which is too autonomous will result in people leaving, and generally being unable to work within organisational structures. On the other side, organisations which foster dependency encounter stuck or plateaued employees, not able to reach their potential, whereas a laissez-faire handing over of responsibility to individuals can create an incoherent, disengaged, or anarchic work-force. I will give some illustrations of how I have come to think in this way.

Examples from practice: individual competences

An individual executive whom I consult on her organisational strategy works for a global knowledge-based organisation, with responsibilities for developing socially responsible practices across the UK business. This huge organisation has structures which are both traditionally functional, hierarchical and slow moving, across which issues such as developing new markets, workforce planning, operate in much looser, faster and flexible structures – an uneven warp and weft.

Career progression for this executive relies not so much on having a clear path to take her from A to B, but in noticing where and how the balance of interest and power is shifting, say between technical, knowledge creating functions and co-ordinating functions. Consequently, she has to be alert to where opportunities exist for her to create a formal role out of the informal processes and needs of the organisation. Organisationally she is supported in taking responsibility for her career through a devolved professional development budget which she can utilise as she chooses, and a culture which in part supports independence of action and initiative, and in part promotes more referential behaviours, depending on which part of the business you inhabit.

This executive's existing role and organisational agenda provides an entry ticket to functional structures, allowing her to move easily about the system, and she is ideally placed to undertake the kind of predominantly independent activities that career ownership requires. In this sense, she could be regarded as something of a plenipotentiary, attempting to gain the collaboration of other systems within the conference setting in order to progress her work. In doing so, she struggles with the same kind of confusions and lack of solid ground that conference experience illuminates and she is challenged with aligning her agenda with those of her functional colleagues and working with their different time frames and priorities.

Entry to systems, which might support and sustain the kind of knowledge creation necessary for both the business and career ownership, is made harder through the multiple cultures operating in relation to this organisation's different structures. Consequently this executive faces the individual set-backs to collaboration so visible in conference work, such as visiting at the wrong time, struggling to convince others of the importance of her agenda and so on. Developing her awareness of the systemic issues at play, in particular, how she is able to make sense of her encounters with 'the other' is crucial in developing her individual capacities to shape her role, and to create the organisational climate she needs to move in her career.

Examples from practice: organisational features

Participants in a leadership training programme I was involved in piloting for a chemical industry decided to set up an action learning set on how the organisation might improve its capacity to attract, retain and develop high performing staff. The subject was chosen by the participants since their newly globalised structure had resulted in a cutting out of several layers of hierarchy, leaving this particular group feeling that they had nowhere to go. The industry as a whole is suitably competitive in terms of attracting staff, but keeping them is more problematic, and with intellectual property at stake movement within the industry is an expensive practice in a variety of ways.

This was a 'virtual' learning set, working via teleconference for most of the time, in view of the dispersed locations of its participants, with occasional face-to-face meetings. Six members participated, configured as three pairs of managers from each of the key international sites. In the early stages, my experience of the learning set was that it was heavy, burdensome work and I felt myself far from being knowledgeable about group behaviour, or having the skills for which I had been appointed. Technically, the work was challenging, but my intention here is not to go into the issues involved in facilitating a virtual group, nor whether it had sufficient requisite organisation (Jaques, 1989) to help it function, but more to explore some of the resonance with Group Relations conference work that was apparent.

In terms of the description of conference experience I gave earlier, then it would be true to say that I and fellow members felt not only unearthed but tipped into some cyberspace-like quagmire where nobody really had a sense of what we were doing, what was happening and how we might get out of it. Survival, getting through, and creating sufficient leverage around the topic seemed to be the imperative, and a capacity to be curious and explore seemed almost entirely absent. Participants repeatedly said that they had never been in a situation like it. I was slow to realise that these participants were probably for the first time in this organisation (and perhaps in their lives) in a group with no defined leader, a task but no clearly defined means of undertaking it, and an outcome that they couldn't envisage. It all had to be created.

It seemed to me that as time went on, the pairs from the international locations began to work in quite a differentiated way. One pair particularly concerned about protocol was reluctant to cross boundaries – both the boundary between scientific staff, and human resource staff whom they needed to access, and the boundary between different levels of the hierarchy. Another pair was sensitive to the issue of inclusion, and wanted to be sure that they justly represented their colleagues, possibly to the exclusion of their own needs. Yet another pair, whilst equally troubled by the dynamics of the learning set, found it easier to get out and about and gather data, and enjoyed networking around the theme.

I came to see this learning set as something of a representatives group (Miller & Rice 1967). Since formation of group identity was slowed by its virtual nature, then back-home ways of doing things remained pervasive, and it seemed likely that this small learning set was largely operating as an 'inter-group' influenced by different cultures in the mind, in relation to both the task in hand, and to preferred ways of doing things within their own international locations.

A face-to-face meeting, some two-thirds of the way through the learning set, provided the opportunity to explore the experience in a more open and authentic way. Significantly, a member realised that the very experiences they had had were curiously mirroring the characteristics of many staff within the function globally, and more particularly related to the very skills that they had highlighted in their research, as being essential to managing one's own career, namely the capacity to work across organisational boundaries, to determine one's own learning needs and the ability to authorise oneself to pursue them. Although I had spoken many times about mirroring, for this group of mainly scientific professionals, this was a turning point.

This was a company sensitive to opportunity, and to how open and shut its doors were for career progression. But it became clear, that in the business of career ownership, these participants were not all starting on a level playing field. Their capacities to develop competencies to manage and own careers were strongly influenced both by the division of tasks between sites over time and by the consequent development of cultures around how this work was achieved.

Mutuality and inter-dependence

This leads me to the issue of mutuality and interdependence. It seems to me that in considering both the individual strengths required and the facilitative environment needed, workers need to be supported in managing their careers both through the acquisition of skills and competencies and through the organisation's own examination of their working practices and the extent to which they foster dependency or autonomy. This is not an easy thing to do. Particularly in dispersed organisations where centralised HR and support structures are crucial to organisational outcomes, systems and procedures are designed to provide help to operational staff, to reduce demands and stress, and to maximise resources and learning to ease the task. This often means doing things for people in a reliable and timely way. Creating an environment which allows for individuals to find their own way, to learn from experience including the capacity to make mistakes, flies in the face of efficiency and seems, and inevitably is, a risk to bottom-line delivery.

Conference experience bears this out. Administrators who encourage participants' self-organisation around limited resources, and consultant staff who will not immediately answer questions, or fill a gap created by the anxiety of not-knowing, are rarely popular, and are frequently experienced as withholding and anti-achievement. Only a careful holding to role and the learning intended will make this stance a manageable or palatable one for staff, when managing, teaching or offering prior knowledge is more socially acceptable. How much harder in lived organisational life, when the pressure is on.

The behaviour possible within an experiential educational event, and that required in organisational life are two different things, but I raise this by way of illustrating the difficulty of moving organisational cultures away from those which foster relations of dependency to those which are able to allow for greater autonomy. The notion of mutuality comes in here. Workers need to risk an autonomy which can tolerate their own needs for dependence upon all that an organisation can provide for them, whilst organisations have to risk a level of involvement with workers that can allow for more independence of thinking and action, whilst maintaining efficiency. However that risk is encountered, a sense of loss is inevitable, and anxiety a reality.

As with the chemical industry and its diverse international cultures, so the task of the organisation, and the extent to which it has to manage risks on behalf of society becomes an inevitable element in this kind of mutual consideration. Sectors in which the range of options available for individual workers are constrained by management of such risk, or powerfully regulated industries like the food and drugs industry, face considerable tensions in trying to facilitate greater creativity and autonomous thinking amongst its workers, in the face of prescriptive modes of organisation.

Conference learning: self vs. organisation

I have so far considered learning from conference work which has its application at an organisational level. However, feedback from conference participants frequently is that much of the learning from conference work is about one's self and one's own capacity to manage anxiety. The very subject of career development in the examples from practice given earlier, is complex, easily evoking personal feelings of success or failure and influencing individuals' capacities to see a desired future.

In the action learning set previously outlined, participants worked with checklists of what they valued as good career opportunities which would encourage them to stay. Increased travel, potential to have secondments into other areas of the business, access to further education and so on, all had limited appeal to this group of highly educated international scientists, whilst recognisable status, envisaged salary, and autonomy to invest in their specialist field were high. This division of 'perks' it seemed to me, related to the known, rather than the unknown, and the known also that relates to reliable and secure structures within a hierarchy. Within an unsettled economy and risky product market, a hierarchical career progression seemed at the minimum to provide a level of containment that might otherwise be missing.

Clearly this is not the case for all. Different occupational groupings, and individuals at different life stages, import their own capacities for security and risk, which come together in how organisations are structured. However, I am suggesting that the need for

containment around the industry or sector task emerges as a significant feature in the way individuals can manage their career port-
folios, and adds a further dimension to the conscious and
unconscious infrastructures seen in organisational cultures.

If I look at what it takes to manage my own career, (and those of
others that I am helping with this) then I know I have to relate to
myself as something of a 'holding company', that is that I have to
provide myself with the kind of structure to examine what I am
doing in its broadest sense, and to contain the anxieties inherent in
the work. As Shapiro (1965) says of autonomy, 'it is predicated upon
the ability to abstract, to separate oneself from others, to "objectify the
world" '. This kind of behaviour is clearly at tension with intra-
personal, social and epistemological desires to 'subjectify' the world,
to be involved, to belong, as the earlier example of the women and
their networking experience illustrated.

Regardless of the kind of contract by which I am employed, I have
to manage my investment in work, and what it means to me. I have
to be sufficiently engaged with my work, but also distanced from it
so as to see that I have choices about what I can do. These
behaviours, it seems to me, link with the emergence of agency and
will in human development, and in particular, how processes of
separation and individuation have been experienced and managed.

These primary dynamics will be different for different people at
different times in their lives, but issues of how to manage needs for
inclusion, belonging, and reward, in the face of exclusion, alienation
and a less stratified notion of success are central to the task of
managing more fluid, opportunistic career trajectories.

To summarise

I have presented ideas around the application of Group Relations
conference work, in suggesting transitional frameworks which
encourage active enquiry and experimental engagement in organisational life. Case examples have shown a specific application to
the issues both individuals and organisations must grapple with
in managing the social trend and organisational imperative for
individuals to take ownership of their careers.

I have also suggested how managing a career portfolio, which requires managing one's self with greater autonomy, generally requires both an engagement with and a distancing from one's own work, and capacity to use the security structures of the organisation to allow greater mobility. It also requires an organisational culture which can foster interdependence, and an examination of ways in which its core business, structures and processes can influence its position on a dependency to autonomy continuum.

In this sense I am proposing a return to the concept of the socio-technical system, a system of work which allows for the social and emotional needs of the worker to be aligned along with industry and sector technology. If individuals are to work as self-regulating, self-organising individuals, then the socio-technical balance requires a shift, one that is away from positions of independence or autonomy to a more mutually derived interdependence.

Acknowledgements

I wish to thank Judy Ritter for her post-workshop communications and Amy Fraher for her questions.

CHAPTER SIX

Surfacing the ecology of public school organisations

The centrality of groups and their dependency container

Carl Mack, Jr

An organisational dynamic

C onsider the following dynamic, which describes an on-going set of behaviours endemic to the public school enterprise.

- The district's failures are highlighted through achievement results on standardised tests. This triggers certain forms of action that tend to prevail.
- The district and foundations commission a university or private study. Community partners are sought and formed. Individual schools and children/students are identified and 'sensational-ised' (either for 'beating the odds' or being failures).
- Funds are demanded, raised and spent.
- These efforts include the customary blaming and anger, includ-ing the students and families in question, the teachers and, oftentimes, the superintendent (and his or her administrative team).
- Promising programmes are developed and implemented with exciting results for small numbers of students in selected schools.

- These efforts comfort us for a while, yet little or no innovation occurs and no significant rise in the achievement of the (targeted) students takes place.

This set of behaviours is repetitive and cyclical to the extent that it has become predictable (Powell & Barber, 2004). As a public school superintendent, I am familiar with this organisational behaviour through participant observation, management and engulfment. This troublesome dynamic affects leadership in the provision of educational service to all children in general, and, specifically to African-American children and their families. This dynamic emerges when the community raises issues about the school district's behaviour and intensifies when student academic performance is the primary focus. And, it seems to appear at its most intense level when 'students of colour' or black students are the focus. At the emotional level, middle-class communities are 'shocked' that middle-class black students are not performing at the same level as their white counterparts. Low-income communities are 'outraged' that black students are not doing well on the (white-derived) standardised tests (that measure academic performance).

The purpose of this paper is to examine this behaviour from an ecological point of view, which argues that the core component of the public school organisational ecology is that of groups. The primary task of public schools – the education of students – is conducted through groups that are 'alive' with the dynamics both seen (conscious) and unseen (subconscious and unconscious). Thus, in this context the term 'ecology' references groups and group dynamics. The contextual focus is the experiences of African-American students in public schools. The primary questions include: What is it that endows this dynamic (or organisational behaviour) with life? Where does this behaviour derive its energy? How does this behaviour adapt itself to its surroundings and, thus, reproduce itself?

Additional questions of interest are: What roles do children play in the emergence of this phenomenon as an organisational dynamic? Does the unconscious emerge because of the presence of children or that they are the primary focus of the (adult) work group? What basic assumption is made to give expression to the unconscious? What can we do to support learning about this dynamic and how to consult it? Can we use innovations and new research information to assist in the examination of this dynamic through the Tavistock model of Group Relations conferences (Hayden & Molenkamp, 2002)?

This article is organised to address four main themes. The first refines the ecological view by highlighting the centrality of groups to the ecology in public school organisations. The second examines the black student in public schools as a particular point of interest. The third identifies an organisational behaviour (described in the opening of this paper) and its connection to a particular aspect of group dynamics (racism). And, finally, based on these experiences, new directions for further inquiry.

Exploring the ecological context: Groups

The primary group of the school is the classroom, which is composed of students (children) and teacher. Richardson (1967) and Mack (1979) have articulated the value of observing the classroom as a group. These studies emphasise the fact that every school and district as an organisation carries out its primary task – that of educating students – through a group, a classroom. However, other groups assist public schools and districts in accomplishing their primary task of providing educational services to students. These groups constitute an important characteristic of a school's organisational structure and culture. For example, a board of trustees is a group of elected public officials to whom the public entrusts the policy direction of the educational enterprise. Staff members meet as a group to make decisions that affect the direction of the school. The school site council is a (small) group of parents and staff members that provides policy direction to the school. Schools often have management or leadership teams, groups of staff members, including the principal, who assist in the day-to-day management of the school. A grade-level team consists of groups of teachers who teach at the same grade level (e.g., third grade) and come together as a group to develop and maintain curriculum integration across the grade level. These groups meet with regularity and have influence on the direction of a school and district.

The groups are brought together to use the sophisticated skills and competence of the individuals that make up the groups. Such skills and competence are applied to the organisational task the group has been formed to examine and they are often quite conscious of the work task they have been assigned. However, they are rarely aware of the underlying (subconscious or unconscious) dynamics that influence their efforts. These groups also serve as the means for the expression of deeper unconscious issues that are brought into play when the group convenes and attempts to accomplish its task (Bion, 1961; Richardson, 1967). What is the effect of these covert dynamics on a group when a primary task has been established by the organisation? While working on the primary task unconscious dynamics are aggravated and surfaced. Yet, limited efforts are made to manage these covert dynamics as they appear and 'submarine,' sabotage and undermine the efforts to achieve the work task of the group. In highlighting this, my objective is to assist in the shaping of an informed consulting approach using our collective knowledge of groups.

A cultural context

A cultural orientation (Phillips, 1998) affects the way one critiques society and the school system (Shujaa, 1994). One way to understand this is through a comparison of views between two key American cultural ancestors – John Dewey and W. E. B. DuBois. Dewey spoke from a European (American) perspective, while the other, DuBois, was African (American) and spoke from that cultural perspective. For Dewey (1916/1944) the social idea of democracy was important, and he said social change should be determined by the rational thinking of the politically dominant members of the society. He also, unfortunately, avoided discussing the matter of oppressed peoples' challenge to that power.

DuBois focused on the cultural conflict in America and its impact on the African-American cultural identity (Shujaa, 1994). He posed a powerful set of questions and challenges to African-Americans: When we become equal American citizens, what will be our aims and ideals, and what will we have to do with selecting these aims and ideals? Are we to assume that we will simply adopt the ideals of

Americans and become what they are or want to be and that we have in this process no ideals of our own? Will we take on the culture of white Americans, doing as they do and thinking as they think? (DuBois, 1973). Shujaa (1994) paraphrases DuBois' position quite accurately, noting that he considered the cultural assimilation of blacks into the politically dominant culture in America to be unacceptable. He saw a clear dilemma for African-Americans – refuse to go to school, or go to school and run the risk of becoming alienated from the African-American cultural community (p. 29).

While Dewey and DuBois were members of the same society, they related to different primary cultural groups. This is an essential element that speaks to the root cause of the achievement gap between black students and the 'norm.' Two cultural groups exist; both produce citizens of America with one having an historical subordinate relationship to the other. Those who work in the Tavistock tradition will recognise the inherent dynamics of the inter-group when these two cultural traditions are brought together in any group context.

The ecological approach is an important and useful tool to examine and identify the underlying issues that affect the achievement performance of black students. However, we need to be clear about the process of the ecology that defines the educational environment of black students. Many of the comments black parents make about *their* experience can be captured by the metaphor of prey and predator. The black child/student is the prey and his or her educational process is the predator.

If this is too harsh, then one might consider the history of African-Americans that includes: Maafa (disaster) the dehumanising circumstance that includes the middle passage and slavery; the black codes that resulted in death if slaves were taught to read; lynching in the United States until 1953; the separate but equal edict of the U. S. Supreme Court (*Plessy v. Ferguson* 1896) which ruled that the state's obligation to provide equal protection under the law was fulfilled by separate but equal facilities; and the 1954 *Brown v. Board of Education* decision that had little or no effect on the achievement gap. In fact, twenty years later, Williams (1974) reported 'a gap between Blacks and whites beginning in kindergarten and increasing through high school.' Nearly fifty years later we are here again discussing the matter of an educational gap.

While brief, this historical kaleidoscope gives some idea as to the depth of the problem (of the achievement gap) and the historical length of its existence. The point is, an ecological view must be accurate in its depiction and description of the dynamics at play. For example, the matters of prejudice, racism, and the pedagogy built on this prejudice/racism are an integral part of the (educational) ecology. That is, through the educational system, the white society negatively affects the African-American child's mind-body growth. This occurs through the nature of the various educational environmental settings or groups, which help determine these children's academic and social growth. Issues such as inconsistency, frightening treatment, distrust, devaluation by others, and mislabelling (overtly or covertly) integral to the group evoke self-devaluation, distrust, negative behaviour, interpersonal difficulties and, thus, poor performance (Mack, 1979, 1981). If not poor performance, then the child/student exhibits a level of performance that is not commensurate with expected, actual or potential capacity. Being black in America and a student in its educational system entails being exposed to highly stressful experiences, triggered primarily by the fact of biogenetic and culture-based differences (Azibo, 1989, 1991).

When dealing with issues of individual or organisational racism, Cooper and Mack (2003) have noted that consultants must be ready to identify racial difference and hatred. They must recognise that there is always more to a system than racial differences, acknowledge the policy and practices vs. examining feelings in-depth dilemma, examine the polarity about incentives for change related to racial hatred and racism, and, when appropriate, promote the Group Relations conferences as a training ground for examining the varying contexts, complexities and intensity of the race issue.

The role of unconscious processes in educational transformation

It is critical to note that some outstanding and valuable analyses have been made regarding the problems of schools and the achievement gap from sociological, anthropological and educational perspectives (Akoto, 1994; Darling-Hammond, 1997; Fine, 1994; Hillard, 1991; Meier, 1995; Tyack & Cuban, 1995). Unfortunately, no matter how valuable or insightful the results, the impact on the achievement gap has been sporadic and, perhaps, negligible at best. Following the lead of Powell & Barber (2004) and their work through Harvard, Columbia Teacher's College, Bank Street School, and the University of San Diego, new developments spark interest in the role of unconscious processes in educational transformation and school improvement.

The dynamics described above are important because they are symbolic of the 'unconscious processes in educational transformation.' Powell and Barber (2004) suggest that educational change and/or transformation is 'full' with unconscious processes. To highlight their view, they make three assumptions about the unconscious and educational transformation:

1. Schools and school systems are cultural symbols and enactments of our own experiences as children, our feelings about children as a group and our feelings about the future.
2. Educational institutions carry tremendous *affect* – strong feelings, deep values, and matters of the heart. Some of this strong affect is what children and their families normally bring into their relationships with schools and this intense affect is projected into schools.
3. What appear to be 'failures' in education are actually extreme and unconscious attempts to protect us from the anxiety stirred by the conflicts in American education. A twisted decipherable logic occurs in both our difficulties in schools and our resistances to improving them with dramatic splitting maintaining a costly stability.

They further argue that the dynamics highlighted by their hypotheses are visibly at work through the interplay of 'conflict and anxiety' and 'anxiety and social defences.'

These authors are clearly working from a 'psychodynamic' point of view. They, on one hand, argue that educators (parents and professionals) 'know' that something deeper is at play in the intense resistance and response to their change efforts; yet, they do not have a systematic method for inquiring or interpreting the phenomenon that they encounter. On the other hand, the authors observe that while the psychoanalytically oriented clinicians and consultants have a method for exploring these unconscious, covert processes, they often do not 'know' the politics or culture of educational transformation or school improvement. Through their work and research in urban schools Powell and Barber have begun to build a conceptual and working bridge between these two groups.

Viewing the ecological approach in this way suggests that 'normal' organisational decision-making presents a substantial challenge to the equitable treatment of African-American students. Here the practical problem is bringing to conscious awareness these subjective decision-making systems that are already in place within the educational ecology. This is especially difficult for jobs and roles in which intangible qualities such as interpersonal skills, creativity, and ability to make sound judgments under conditions of (cultural) uncertainty are critical (Krieger, 1995), e.g., teacher, educational manager, and educational leader. If not taken into account, this subtle system and its operation may go on, largely unnoticed and, thus, unaddressed. So, 'yes' to an ecological approach that takes into account the extent to which organisational dynamics adversely affect the performance of black students in disproportionate ways on measurable, seemingly objective outcomes.

The provocation and the organisational behaviour

While the above expresses an intense concern about the achievement gap of black students, the ultimate goal is providing support and consultation to public school organisations as they go through change and transformation processes. Typically, in analysing its test results the public school district determines that the black student is performing at a lower rate then its white or Asian student counterparts. Here, the focus is not the political reactions by the various segments of the community, but the organisational response and what it represents in the context of group and organisational life. The method or lens to sharpen this focus is the Tavistock perspective (Hayden & Molenkamp, 2002).

Using the work of Bion (1961), Miller & Rice (1967), Richardson (1967), Rioch (1971), and Banet & Hayden (1977), group and human relations conferences have been conducted at graduate schools of education in courses on leadership, group dynamics and urban education. In addition, these conferences have been an integral part of many urban institutes and networks. Many of the participants are faced with almost paralysing conflicts and inequities in the schools and districts under their leadership. However, the conference work and application cases concluded that what is or was feared most offered educators the greatest opportunities for learning and substantive change.

With this perspective, 'dependency container' is one way to conceptualize this organisational dynamic or behaviour. This behaviour contains the organisation's anxiety and its efforts to defend itself against very complex and deeply unconscious dynamics provoked by groups. Its defence is, in part, its inability to manage these complex unconscious dynamics that go unattended in all of the groups at work within its organisational system. The dependency container has as its essential aim the attainment of security and protection. The organisation acts *as if* it must protect itself from the implementation of a 'manageable' strategy that has the support of those who assume leadership roles. The partner groups of parents or community often act *as if* they are incompetent or lacking in skills, hoping that the situation will be solved either by a leader, the power and clarity of the research, or their political attacks against the organisation. As an expression of the underlying hostility and disappointment, the actions of the various groups, including organisational leadership, often 'kill off' anything that has the capacity to meet the various demands. This includes the leaders, the energy of the research, and the political agenda. In this case, the dependency container is produced by the anxiety of the participants' fear of being engulfed by the unknown forces in the groups and organisation, particularly those associated with racism and racial hatred. The defensive actions consist of the maintenance of mindless confusion precluding any examination of facts and/or reality related to these deep feelings and negative beliefs that are left unexamined.

Specifically, the 'dependency container' is composed, in part, of:

- The feelings, cultural symbols and enactments that are evoked in the adults as they interact with the schools and school systems. These represent their symbolic, political and psychological investment in schools that contains matters such as race, racial hatred and white supremacy (Hillman, 1986).

- The strong feelings, deep values and 'matters of the heart' that children and families bring with them to schools and the district reflect their earliest experiences of authority and leadership in their family and schooling.
- The extreme and unconscious attempts of protection from the anxiety stirred by the conflicts of children and adults working in the various groups of the schools and district.

These are some of the underlying or deeper issues that are contained by and help shape this organisational dynamic or behaviour referred to as a 'dependency container.'

Places to go

Using this metaphor gives us something concrete with which to work as it relates to the Tavistock model of group and organisational consultancy. This dependency container mirrors the ingredients of the dependency basic assumption and underlying problems that consists of 1) the dynamics individuals bring into their effort in working with schools, 2) the deeper unconscious dynamics provoked by small-, medium- and large-sized group work, and 3) the threats to individual and collective cultural identity provoked by these groups in their organisational system or contexts. This suggests that the poor performance of black students, while a problem, is also the symptom of deeper organisational problems. These problems require simultaneous work at the functional individual level as well as at the group and organisational levels.

These are the deeper forces that emerge and are provoked when young children are present in the group and/or the object of the 'working' group's attention. The point is that the human mind has a dynamic hidden mental life that absorbs images and complex information, processes it on simple and apparently sophisticated levels, is capable of subtle perceptions that influence behaviour, and has a deep, implicit memory of important and repeated situations. Bynum (1999) argues that unconscious primordial racial memories unfold different psychological and psycho-spiritual (Bynum, 2000) field dynamics from the intra-psychic, interpersonal and systemic model of influence and causality. Since the concept 'unconscious' is central to the theory and practice of Tavistock, this has implications both for consulting groups in educational organisations as well as for future Group Relations conference designs. The task is to bring the unconscious into our scientific and historical grasp for use to reframe a central construct to Tavistock work.

The public school system has a unique and often vicarious position in the society. It is given the 'trust' of socialising children into productive citizens of the larger American culture and society. However, a Euro-centred cultural perspective shapes both educational orthodoxy as well as the level of care and trust found in the educational process. When young children of other cultures are involved, the intensity of parental concern is high and takes many and varied forms when their children experience personal and institutional racist behaviours. On the one hand, the organisation's ecology works at a pace that promotes slow change (which contributes to a certain level of safety) and produces a wide range of academic outcomes for children of all backgrounds. Yet, on the other hand, this same system's behaviour contains factors that produce 'savage inequalities' for large numbers of students.

Tavistock conferences provide powerful experiential opportunities to examine these issues; particularly, the work of the unconscious as it is provoked by the presence of young children in the group or as the focus of group work. Clearly, the problem of the dependency container is not solely one of interpersonal dynamics, behaviour and communications. These stereotyped beliefs and prejudices about one another are embedded into the public school organisation, operate outside of our attention, and are not always attributable to an individual's actions. They are systemic in nature.

The conceptual framework of Tavistock traditions

Tavistock traditions that were based on providing consultation to groups are now useful in consulting to the complexities of organisational dynamics. In particular, the Tavistock tradition provides ideas relating to the dependency container – illuminating that seemingly invisible relationship of individuals to the various groups in which they participate and these groups' relationship to the larger organisational system that contains them. Ideally, the problem solving or consultant intervention must make these multiple-levelled links visible. That is, consultations must work on three levels simultaneously. An intervention on one level, the individual, must find an impact or link on the other two levels, e.g., the group and organisation.

Changing organisational demands require consultancy practices where working in and with groups directly effects organisational change (Neumann & Hirschhorn, 1999). This approach shapes consultations that work with both the visible and invisible aspects of group and organisational life. It consists of 1) being derived from a human relations paradigm, 2) providing an opportunity to study behaviour as it occurs, 3) providing the opportunity to learn about behaviour at individual and group levels of analysis, 4) increasing one's awareness of the self in groups, and 5) increasing effective and responsible behaviour in groups.

Holvino (2003) observed eight integrating behaviours that are embedded in four conceptual tools, referred to as links, linking, or the process of attending – paradoxes, polarities, levels of analysis, and linking across differences. This is referred to as the 'third way' of consulting to groups and organisations. She proposes that evolving a third way involves reframing the *paradox* so that the group finds the connection embedded in the apparent contradiction. In the case of *polarities*, the third way requires attending to and bringing in the opposite of an articulated polarity in the group, e.g., overt and covert, progressive and regressive dynamics. The *levels of analysis* approach promotes consultancy that involves paying attention to all the different levels of a system, highlighting one or another type of interaction or system phenomena when addressing the purpose of the consultancy. Finally, linking across differences refers to finding the frame or intervention that makes sense of the polarities, paradoxes, and levels of analysis.

It is suggested that public school organisational behaviour can be seen as a 'container' for deep symbolic unconscious matter. Some sort of hierarchy always emerges as the conservative or liberal force in the community. Yet, some fundamental educational orthodoxy maintains its identity despite the constant changes and variations that beset it. If there were no powerful orthodoxy advocate, the public school organisation might disintegrate. In fact, some organisational orthodoxy seems essential. Its existence and related unconscious phenomena promote the emergence of what we have called a dependency container behaviour forcing us to examine, intervene and consult at various levels simultaneously. That is, for example, as we intervene at the organisational level, the intervention must also address group and individual issues. By reintegrating the traditions of organisational and group consultancy, we can develop a 'third way' that produces a consultant stance that impacts the three levels simultaneously.

Summary

I have suggested that while the ecological approach can be a useful and successful model for conceptualising the achievement gap exhibited by black students, it needs to be dynamically shaped to include the centrality of groups and the unconscious processes that will occur during any transformative effort. If, for example, when transformation reaches the stage in which research is necessary to clarify issues of the students and their families, then a concomitant level of 'action research' should be used to clarify the unconscious processes that *will* take place at the individual, group and organisational levels (Klein, Gabelnick, & Herr, 1998; Hirschhorn, 1988; Richardson, 1967; Schein, 1992; Stein, 1995; Wheatley, 1992).

While working on the unconscious is not a panacea, history suggests that changes in our public school organisational interventions must occur in order to be effective in improving education for all children in general and specifically for black students. And, these changes must help us understand and frame it 'as natural that strong feelings will arise.' When the organisational dynamic (the dependency container) emerges, we must implement not only an innovation or a research based intervention, but a (deep) process that gives children and adults (parents, guardians, teachers and administrators) the opportunity and support to work through the anxiety and conflict that accompanies any transformation in structure, purpose or process. To change the current educational system we have perpetuated since the early days of schooling requires some 'internal' organisational work that recognises our role in the injustice of its effect on many students and determines the benefits of changing it.

CHAPTER SEVEN

Contradictory demands and basic assumptions

A case study on role taking in a university clinic

Siv Boalt Boëthius

There seems to be a general assumption in the working environment that available resources, such as staff, leadership, finance, technology, etc., are used in a constructive way; that there is a capacity to develop adequate structures and boundaries in the work context and that there is a capacity for containment. However, in situations characterised by external or internal threats or conflicts, unconscious emotional strains or basic assumptions (Bion, 1961) often tend to emerge 'work-group activity is obstructed, diverted and on occasion assisted, by certain other mental activities that have in common the attribute of powerful emotional drive' (ibid. p.146). In order to continue and develop the work, it is necessary to understand, cope with and integrate the basic assumptions cultures that arise. As pointed out by Menzies Lyth (1988) and others, organisations tend to develop different types of basic assumptions depending on the kind of work they have to perform. For example, a common dilemma in a university clinic, where both research and training are carried out in addition to treatment, is that these different types of work evoke different kinds of basic assumptions, which tend to clash.

The primary task of a university is to provide academic education and research, in which the general basic assumption is 'fight-flight'. People fight for their ideas, fight to get students to do their work, fight for grants, etc. Often there is overt or covert competition with colleagues, which can be stimulating and creative, but which is also destructive and can cause fragmentation and fear. The anxiety of failure, for example in the exams or of not being approved or promoted or one's research not being up to standard, contributes to such reactions. The gratification linked to working at a university is primarily getting one's work published. Being a good teacher is valuable, but in the eyes of the university it is not enough. In a psychotherapeutic clinic, the work of the individual clinician is based on the capacity to relate to patients and the main basic assumption in a clinic is 'dependency' (Obholzer & Roberts, 1994). Gratification in clinical work is linked to how successful the individual clinician is in achieving dependable working relationships and good treatment results. The staff at a university clinic often experience many dilemmas arising from the contradictory demands of the different tasks that they have to perform. They tend to identify with one or, at most, two tasks, rather than with all. Instead, they need to find ways to integrate clinical treatment, training and research, which implies developing strategies that can combine and make use of the different cultures and basic assumptions underlying the work. They also need to be aware that these demands sometimes cannot be combined, and that it is up to the clinic as a whole to find ways of dealing with this aspect of their work, not just to the individual members of staff.

The above-mentioned dilemmas will be presented through a case study based on my personal experience in a university clinic abroad, which had recently been reorganised following an international evaluation of the research work carried out in the department. The evaluation report showed that there was a lack of systematic use of data based on the actual work at the clinic, and that the output was too low. One effect of the reorganisation was that the clinic lost some of its previous independence. Another was that the clinical staff had to engage in regular research projects in order to keep their jobs. To assist the adaptation to this new situation, it was decided to invite a visiting professor for one year, with the aim of increasing the scientific output of the institution in general, and especially that of clinical personnel. When I was invited, I received a secondary request from the head of the university clinic, who expressed a wish for consultation due to her difficulties with the staff and the management of the clinic, and also as a consequence of this change in the general policy.

The background

This university clinic was organised like most other clinics that provide psychotherapy. It can select patients depending on available staff resources, and with regard to specific projects, in which patients can be asked to take part. One such project was group psychotherapy for young adults, another concerned eating disorders and a third focused on early childhood problems. The staff members were expected to work as clinicians with the patients – children, adolescents and adults – through diagnostics and psychotherapy, as university teachers providing supervision and seminars, and as researchers, mainly using data generated at the clinic. The overall aim in this chapter is to describe the dilemmas caused by contradictory demands and how fight-flight and dependency behaviour characterised the work and the organisational culture of the clinic. The focus is on how I, as a new member of staff on a time-limited mandate, could make use of the different roles I could take on or was given by the staff and the head of the clinic. Initially, my work could be described as consisting of two roles – researcher and consultant. However, it soon became evident that my experience also as a clinician (as a child and adolescent psychotherapist and a psychoanalyst) played an important part in the daily work, as they expected me to understand their dilemmas.

An important tool in this work was my previous experiences in Group Relations conferences. In these, one learns about the importance of sticking to one's role also in complex, sometimes quite chaotic situations, and of providing the conditions for containment and a space for reflection as well as the experience of shifting roles in a flexible organisation. Furthermore, they also include learning about how the structural factors, such as delegation of authority and boundary issues, could be dealt with, together with the financial aspects and technology etc. My earlier experiences as head of a similar organisation in my own country were of great importance too. I had also worked for many years as a researcher at Stockholm University with various types of organisational and clinical projects. The combination of all these experiences helped me to understand what the head of the clinic and the members of staff had to deal with. On a practical level, my agreed assignment was to take up this job on a daily basis for half a year, which included living in the city during this time, followed by a number of follow-up visits afterwards over a six month period.

During the first part of the assignment, I was seen as a member of staff with different tasks, which developed day-by-day and my role shifted depending on the requirements. For obvious reasons, the second part of the assignment implied less involvement in the everyday life of the clinic. This also meant that my different roles were more clearly defined according to the different tasks as well as the type of co-operation that was implied for each specific task. This paper is based on case material and the permission to publish the material has kindly been given by the head of the clinic.

The project

The project in which I was involved can be divided into three phases: the first two during the first six months and the third during the following six months. During the first phase, I mainly observed and got acquainted with the people, and the organisation of the work of the department and of the university clinic. The second phase implied more direct interaction with specific projects, which also meant getting to know individual persons and their way of working, as well as taking a more active part in the decision-making during meetings, and attending two-day policy meetings, etc. The third phase consisted of five visits, each of two to three days during the spring and the following autumn, during which I worked on specific targets. I took part in several two-day policy meetings, initiated and was directly involved in some research projects, kept in contact with the head of the clinic and I reported back to the staff and to the head of the department.

Phase one

At the beginning, my role was an observer one, similar to the way Hinschelwood and Skogstad (2000) describe the role of the observer in an organisational setting, based on the role of observer in Infant Observations (Bick, 1964). This meant being present and as attentive as possible, 'absorbing' the types of interactions and trying to reflect on and understand what was going on, without taking any actions or getting involved in the various processes. On my first day, during a conference for all the staff, I was asked what I wanted to know about the clinic and I replied that I was interested in how the clinical work was organised. This turned out to be important, since most of the staff thought that they were expected to present their research projects, or lack of them. By my concentrating on the role of the clinician (unconsciously), I felt that the staff became more open towards me and less suspicious. During this period, I met all the clinicians and received information about their work and research projects. The approach during this part of my work can be described as performing a dual role, that of the clinician and the researcher, where the role of clinician was the more important one.

In my role as consultant, I was asked to take part in various administrative and clinical meetings. They accepted that I did not want to be particularly active in expressing any opinions during this phase. I had to gain sufficient understanding of the organisation as a whole and its different subsystems before I could get involved in concrete projects. This initial phase mainly in the observer role gave me many opportunities to listen to various narratives concerning the clinic and its previous history. It was evident that it was an institution with a long and complex history, with several fairly traumatic processes, which sometimes seemed to be acted out during conferences and in other situations. These processes, rooted in the earlier history, were remembered well by some staff members, who felt that the importance of this history was denied, since the interest of the other staff in sharing past experiences was limited.

It was obvious that my arrival had been well prepared by the university clinic and that I was welcome, although there was some lack of clarity from the university's administrative section before the final decision that I should come was made. I had a post box with my name on from the first day, a large comfortable room, and somebody had put flowers on my table.

Phase two

During the second phase, the differentiation between the roles I took up became more complex, and it became important to be clear about when I was taking on the role of the clinician, the role of the researcher or the role of the consultant. It also became obvious that different members of staff saw me in different ways. For some, I was perceived partly as a threat and they tended to avoid me, while others related to me as somebody who might be able to help and support them. Although these more negative perceptions changed over time, for some members of staff, the idea of having somebody coming in from the outside, to whom a lot of information and also power was given, was not regarded as altogether positive. However, there was some evidence that the time limit of my stay was important in order to make my contribution more acceptable.

As clinician and university teacher, I took part in intake-conferences, discussed assessment methods, scrutinised the organ-isation of the data in client files and also held seminars for the students. As a researcher, I discussed concrete projects and took part in strategic decisions aimed at developing a policy for the develop-ment of research at the clinic over a period of time. As mentioned above, one of the dilemmas was that there were few projects, which were based on the clinical treatments carried out at the clinic; another one was that few projects involved more than one person.

As a consultant, I was asked to meet different subgroups within the staff. Often these groups had difficulties with their work situ-ation or with the head or the rest of the clinic. These requests were defined in terms of consulting with or to a group, so I was able to take on the role of the consultant with a defined aim and organisa-tional frame for these meetings. In the role as consultant, I also met the head of the clinic on a continuous basis to provide feedback.

Phase three

At this point, after having left the clinic and the daily work, my role clearly became more focused on the dual role of researcher and consultant. As a researcher, I took an active part in some projects, which involved discussions about designing new studies, developing methods for the data collection and processing, and I also took part in the actual writing of articles.

During this phase, my role as a consultant became more clearly established than before. An important factor of this process was a 'reflection session' towards the end of a two-day policy meeting with all the staff, which I was asked to chair. At this session, I presented a hypothesis about the contradictory demands on the staff as a whole group and on individual staff members with regard to clinical work versus research. The different organisational cultures, partly as a consequence of their different basic assumptions – dependency and fight-fight culture – were recognised, and this allowed a number of associations. It was also obvious that the possibility of shifting the discussion from concrete details and personal issues to a meta-level where general phenomena could be distinguished had a stimulating effect.

At the next policy meeting, the strategies that had been decided upon seemed to work well. The main topic discussed was the organisation of the clinic as a whole, and the dilemma of combining clinical work and research. Another concern was how to use the demand for clinically based research projects more constructively, and how to create more open relationships within the clinic itself and with the outside world by developing project teams, presenting projects at conferences, etc. It had become evident that the clinic had been fairly isolated for a long time and that there was now an increased interest in promoting greater communication with the outside world. During the last two meetings, these reflections were discussed and most of the suggested strategies seemed to have been implemented in a constructive way.

A theoretical frame of reference

Contradictory demands and cognitive dissonance

One way of understanding the type of contradictory demands involved in the well-known dilemma of clinical work versus research as described above is by using the concept of cognitive dissonance (Festinger, 1957). The idea of cognitive dissonance is that when groups are faced with contradictory demands which they are unable to integrate emotionally, they tend to choose the safest and most familiar alternative. The chosen alternative will be emotionally charged and arguments will be found to support the view that this or that way is the best solution. However, this way of managing experiences and situations that evoke anxiety, insecurity or conflicts tend to become a habit over time. The flexibility and possibility of identifying alternative solutions or new perspectives tends to vanish, the curiosity about the 'unknown' diminishes and creativity gets lost.

The development of this habitual way of dealing with anxiety-loaded issues connected to the core content of work of an organisation can be described in terms of social structures as a defence against anxiety (Jaques, 1955). There is also some evidence indicating that individual members of an organisation use the social structures that develop, as a defence against their own anxiety. Although it is the individual who feels the anxiety and uses these defences, this kind of defensiveness can also be locked into the social system. As a whole, the system then operates in a way that allows individuals to avoid certain anxieties and conflicts, in particular those that can be awakened by the institution's primary task (Menzies Lyth, 1988).

To a certain extent, the work organisation of the university clinic as a social system can be seen as being characterised by social structures as a defence against anxiety. One source that contributed to this was the unsolved conflicts between sub-units within the staff, due to different attitudes and feelings about how to deal with the demand to engage both in clinical work and research. Another source was unsolved issues about the historical roots of the clinic. There was also, especially at the beginning of my work, a lack of containment, which seemed to invite some destructive challenges of the boundaries, for example the way some conferences were organised. The communication system, in particular with the administrative subsystem, was another area of missing containment, but this changed drastically over time when more regular communications between different subsystems were developed. In general, there was an underlying anxiety and fear about not being up to standard, about not daring to show oneself, neither as a person nor as an institution.

The function of roles

The concept of role can be defined in different ways. For example, it can depend on the focus, which can be either on the psychological dimension of the person taking on a role, or on the interaction with 'others' and the context, mainly a socio-psychological perspective. In this case study, both perspectives were used. One definition from a psychological perspective is described by Reed (1988, pp. 4–5) 'as a mental regulating principle, based on the person's living experience of a complex interaction of feelings, ideas and motivations, which are being aroused by external interactions with a system and is expressed in purposive behaviour'. He describes three dimensions of roles: firstly, they need to be searched for and found, which implies an understanding of the boundaries of the systems. Secondly, they need to be established, which implies an understanding of how the system functions and changes, and finally they need to be taken on, for the benefit of the system and those in it. He also describes that the development of a role and of being in the role is a ceaseless disciplined process and that roles are tools for the management of learning. A role is a formed idea-in-the-mind leading to action as well as to visible behaviours of an inward discipline of knowledge, thoughts, feelings and will.

From a socio-psychological standpoint, roles imply a division of labour among group members, which often helps the achievement of the group's goal, and they constitute an important motivating factor. One of the problems of all groups is to find ways to share work and responsibility among the group members, in order to prevent leaders from being physically, psychologically or cognitively overloaded. A second function of roles is similar to that provided by the normative systems, in that they help to regulate the group's life. Like norms, roles imply expectations about one's own and other's behaviour, and this means that the life of the group becomes more orderly. The emergence of task and social-emotional roles is important, since group members will quickly learn who to look for and they will respond to this person at a certain point in the group's life or in a particular situation. Finally, roles are also a means of our self-definition within the group; they contribute to our sense of identity. A clearly defined role undoubtedly contributes in important ways to our identity. Brown (2000, p. 73) states that 'not knowing who you are or what is expected of you seems to be bad for you'. It is thus important to find a balance between who you are as a person and the role you take on in a specific group or organisational setting.

An added perspective

As an integration with what I have presented as my perspective, it may be useful to include the perspective of the head of the clinic, in order to get a fuller picture of the change process. What follows is based on the description of her experience, which she shared with me towards the end of the first six months of my visit. The idea underlying the clinic head's decision to use a consultant was that she wanted somebody coming in from 'outside'. For her, the consultant should represent 'rationality' and a sense of a 'working ego', as a balance to the irrational processes, projections, alliances, etc. in the organisation. The consultant should be perceived as a sort of a 'third eye', who does not join alliances or undermine work. An interesting question is how long this 'ideal' situation lasts. This probably depends on whether the consultant works 'inside' the organisation or comes in from the 'outside'. To what extent can the consultant maintain his or her neutrality, or does he or she slowly become part of the organisation and of its various alliances and cultural assumptions? And if this happens, does the consultant really shift her or his focus or does the consultant, in time, become the target of projections of the same kind as others have before?

One hypothesis could be that, in the beginning, the consultant has the advantage of being 'new', the outsider. This implies not knowing much about the organisation – neither formally nor informally – but also that of being unknown to the staff members. This itself can stimulate projections and fantasies about almost anything. The primary task of the consultant could be described as assisting in improving the working climate of the organisation, which is stimulating for most staff members. At the same time, the consultant would have to make certain choices and give priority to some tasks over others. This means that the consultant puts specific demands on the staff members and also makes him or herself more visible. Therefore, the consultant cannot avoid becoming increasingly drawn into various groups and organisational processes.

And what happens when the consultant leaves? Can the changes and goals achieved continue to be followed up? Has the work with the consultant left a sufficient impact, or does the institution return to its old way of functioning? In one way, the effect of a consultant's work in an institution can be compared with one of the effects of a therapeutic contact. Just the fact of being in therapy implies a change in the balance between inner psychic forces or conflicts in the person. A similar phenomenon happens when a consultant enters an institution. The question of time is also relevant. How long should a person be in therapy for change to happen? And how long should a consultant work in an institution for change to happen? Obviously, the question cannot be answered in a general way. Just as a fairly short period of therapy can be effective for a well motivated person, the same can occur with a consultancy in a well motivated institution. However, the opposite is also true; if destructive processes are allowed to take over after the consultant has left, the chances of a positive change are very limited.

Discussion

I have described briefly some issues relating to contradictory demands and role-taking when working as visiting professor with a staff group on a time-limited assignment. The setting was a university clinic, where the staff members were torn between the demands from the clinic to produce clinical work and from the university to produce research. The initial request was for me to assist the research and to consult on the work of the clinic, which had gone through a major reorganisation.

With regard to attitudes towards combining research and clinical work, it was evident during the last policy meetings that major changes had been achieved. The polarisation had decreased between those who perceived clinical work as their main task and those who perceived research as their main task. The need to defend one's role as a clinician was less evident and clinical work being the basis for their existence was fully accepted. The open discussion about the two basic assumption cultures: fight-flight and dependency in relation to research and psychotherapy was seen as relevant and helpful.

In addition, there was also a tendency to use pairing as a basic assumption culture. In research, as well as in the caring professions, there is always the hope that something unexpected will crop up to solve a difficult situation and save whatever it is that needs saving. When applying this to the context presented in this paper, the idea of inviting a full-time consultant, who is both a researcher and clinician, could be seen as a way of giving rise to a messianic hope of change. However, to summarise what can be regarded as results in terms of attitudes towards work three years after my intervention, I would say that the development described in this presentation still continues and that research is now focussing more also on the clinical work at the clinic.

In terms of my experience of taking up a role in the university clinic, it is evident that I was able to use my different roles as researcher, consultant and clinician in an interesting way. On the whole, the different roles increased and decreased in importance at different times and in different functions. Using Reed's (1988) description about role-taking, the role of clinician acted as an entrance ticket and had an informal implicit meaning as a way of establishing a common value system. The role of researcher was more official, and maybe therefore was perceived by some as more threatening. And lastly, the role of consultant, mainly to the head of the clinic, had to be established over time through proving myself in the work process.

This transformation of roles can also be described as a form of action research, where the mandate for my participation in the change process was developed and clarified over time. Action research is about assisting the client in practical problem solving and at the same time expanding scientific knowledge, as well as enhancing the competencies of different actors about change. It emphasises collective work, mutual dependence between the researcher and the client as well as the competencies of the individuals involved in the project (Westlander, 2000).

An interesting aspect of this project was that there were few open conflicts, which could not be dealt with one way or the other. I hypothesise that this could be due to the long time-span of the project, so enough shared understanding could be developed with regard to the aim of the work of the clinic and of the system. It was clear that the roles I took on and was given were developed from the close interaction with the members of staff and the head of the clinic in their respective roles. Another important aspect was that the relationships I developed with the people of the clinic were mainly work relationships rather than personal ones, although it was difficult to say if we were aware of this or not.

There was also a general awareness of the risk of, on one hand, giving me too much power and, on the other, perceiving me as a threat, which would lead to avoidance and prevent further development. Although these anxieties and fears existed, there was also a strong motivation to work on this project together. From my perspective, it was a challenge that I appreciated, as in some ways I saw it as a continuation and a development of my previous work. From the perspective of the clinic, in spite of all difficulties and the contradictory demands, there was enough motivation for change and for developing a combination of research and psychotherapeutic and diagnostic work, as demonstrated by the way policy plans and strategies for change were implemented.

Part IV

Researching Group Relations Conferences methodology and outcome

In this section, Lilian Hupkens and Allan Shafer courageously explore outcomes and learning from attendance at Group Relations conferences from different perspectives and levels.

The two authors use different research methodologies for their investigations. Hupkens analyses interviews she conducted in Holland for her Belgirate's presentation, with people in the business world who attended Group Relations conferences in different countries. Shafer's reflections in his paper are based on his own experience in Australia as a member, as consultant, as director and as sponsor.

Both papers emphasise the value of Group Relations conferences and the importance for members' learning both from an individual perspective and in terms of the passion and enthusiasm for this new kind of knowledge. Shafer says 'my personal learning was firstly about individual awareness ... Group Relations work has also equipped me to apply that awareness to thinking divergently about systemic experiences and about how my up-take of roles is shaped by my personal valencies in interaction with organisational dynamics'. Hupkens' interviewees found 'that their whole way of looking at groups of people, their way of seeing things had changed. It was as if they had acquired a new and different pair of spectacles'.

However, they both suggest that it is more complicated to define and delineate the application of Group Relations conferences at an organisational/systemic level, in terms of the transition of organisational/systemic learning from the temporary organisation to the daily environment. It is as if, once outside the boundary of the conference, members are caught in a feeling of isolation and passivity where the energy acquired during the conference as well as the effort in working through their experiences, fades away. Shafer argues that this is also the case for the sponsoring organisations which are not always able to retain learning and to implement the transition from individual to collective learning. He suggests that 'organisational interest', for example, interest in the work of predecessors, can be a way of promoting the building of organisational knowledge in a past, present and future dimension.

The authors say either explicitly or implicitly that 'opening members' eyes' to see new things can also be a 'disadvantage' of Group Relations conferences. Shafer perceives this as subversive learning 'in the way it challenges cultural norms'. Hupkens suggests that increased awareness of the dynamics in the system may make it impossible for some people 'to continue staying in the same workplace'. So, perhaps some of the resistances to learning at an organisational level could be the result of anxieties that these types of assumptions or ideas can cause. Therefore, the challenge for Group Relations practitioners is how to help members make their learning and transformations long lasting in the post-conference phase at both individual and organisational levels.

Hupkens makes an interesting point about the depth of learning, arguing that it should not be assumed that the most powerful emotional experiences during the conferences are those from which members learn most; much 'may be acquired through osmosis' during the conference.

Both papers touch on the issue of the applicability and learning of Group Relations conferences for managers. Hupkens suggests that many managers in the business world today are more sensitive to psychological process, and are therefore more open to learn in a psychodynamic setting. Shafer, in contrast, highlights the struggle between the 'executive' and the 'caring' functions of managers with a clinical background who have been exposed to psychoanalysis.

CHAPTER EIGHT

Multi-level application of Group Relations Conferences learning

Staff, members and sponsoring organizations

Allan Shafer

In a paper exploring the key themes of past major Group Relations conferences run by the Australian Institute of Socio-Analysis I described the development of what I called 'the socio-analytic mind' in Australia. AISA ran Group Relations conferences from 1986 to 2003. Socio-analysis is the activity of exploration, consultancy and action research that combines and synthesizes methodologies and theories derived from psychoanalysis, Group Relations, social systems thinking, organizational behaviour and social dreaming. Among other things, I tried to discern whether particular themes in these conferences might relate to unconscious social anxieties in Australian organizational life. I also wondered whether the conference themes (in addition to the *conscious* motives in their selection) represented, as socio-analytic material, manifestations of *unconscious* social anxieties or concerns in AISA.

In reflecting on that paper in the context of the Belgirate Conference, I realized that I wanted to contribute to the understanding and development of learning from Group Relations conferences that has emerged from Australian ways of working. The late Eric Miller once commented to me on the relative freedom to innovate that he imagined we had in Australia, because of our location so far from

123

the epicentre of Group Relations work in the UK. I believe that Australian conferences have held true to the primary tasks, structures, methodologies and processes of the so-called 'Tavistock tradition' of Group Relations conferences. The peculiarities of Australian culture have distinctively shaped our work and have opened up interesting and adventurous possibilities for applying learning from Group Relations conferences. I refer in particular to our learning – perhaps action-learning – in the development of the methodologies.

In this chapter I address three levels of applied learning: for participants, for staff and for sponsoring organizations – in this case AISA. Much has been written about transference of conference learning and the application of learning for the *individual* (e.g. Reed (1976). I am covering a spectrum: the individual, the group and the organization rather than examining the detailed nature of adult learning in the context of Group Relations.

1. Applied learning for Conference members

My personal *membership* experience of Group Relations conferences was that they were the most significant adult learning encounters I had had, apart from my own psychoanalysis. Conference learning is not therapy: rather it has enabled me to think and to learn in novel, innovative and creative ways about myself, about my own mind, about the dynamics of group and organizational life, and about the nature of authority. Learning about how I took up particular roles in conferences and the application of this learning to my up-take of organizational roles was an educative experience unique to Group Relations conferences.

My interest in the notion of *learning* from Group Relations conferences is reflected in the themes I have selected for some of the conferences that I have directed. For example: *Authority for Learning: a working conference to explore the dynamics of authority, leadership, courage and organizational learning* (1999), and *Learning for Leadership* (in 2003 and 2004). Its also evident in the development of what I called an 'applied' conference for participants who self-identified as 'psychotherapists', entitled *Who am I at work?* (2001). (With acknowledgement to Susan Long from whom this term was borrowed.)

As I have developed as a conference director responsible for the design of conferences, I have had repeatedly to re-evaluate a remark Gordon Lawrence once made to me (when we worked on the staff of an AISA conference in 1991) that *what you learn in Group Relations conferences is how to behave in Group Relations conferences*. The assumptions underlying this position call for exploration.

In their paper on *Modernism and post-modernism in Group Relations*, Gertler and Izod (2004) indicated that 'In this broader field of application we are concerned to maximize the relatedness of conference experience and learning to the everyday experience of members in their workplace, cultural or societal context.' While their primary concerns are about the relevance of Group Relations conferences to *post-modern* organizations, which they suggest evolved for *modern* organizations, they make some points relevant to this exploration of conference learning. In particular, they suggest that:

> Feedback from participants is often that learning is essentially related to individual awareness even though the focus of consultation is usually systemic, and aimed at enhancing organizational awareness. Members speak of being at odds with the methodology, role(s), and stance of the staff members, describing scenarios in their everyday workplaces that de-emphasize hierarchy, where they engage in multiple tasks, and where relationships with managers are more accessible. Boundaries between systems are seen as more fluid, and subject to constant flux and change.

My personal learning *was* firstly about 'individual awareness'. However the frameworks provided by Group Relations have also equipped me to apply that awareness to thinking divergently about my systemic experiences and about how my up-take of roles is shaped by my personal valencies in interaction with organizational dynamics.

The applicability of learning from 'traditional' Group Relations conferences may not always adequately assist conference participants to think divergently about their own contemporary organizational settings and may indeed provide them with frameworks which are now less relevant and perhaps even erroneous. However, while the structure of post-modern organizations may be different, the impact of different or changing organizational structures on the nature of group dynamics and Group Relations may need to be thought about. Simultaneously, I think that many contemporary organizations continue to operate with 'modern' rather than 'post-modern' structures and processes, and themselves may not equip their members to think and act in post-modern ways about their operations.

These are critically important considerations which we, as conference promoters must examine and evolve, if Group Relations is to thrive as a relevant learning platform in a post-modern world. Despite these considerations – perhaps even misgivings – I would like to describe more concretely some of the emerging processes for application of conference learning in Australia. I particularly want to discuss Review and Application Events and Follow-up Programmes.

1.1. Review and application

Australian conferences have almost always had various forms of Review, Reflection and/or Application Groups. These events are usually located at points in the programme when participants have both sufficient and evolving conference experience to work on. They occur in small consistent peer groups with a consultant. The staff has allocated group membership around similarity of work role or issues; sometimes members self-select groups or consultants to work with, though group membership is always required to be stable. It seems worth exploring whether there are differences in learning related to differences in group formation. However, the fact that such data has not been collected is probably an indication of one of the failures of learning in organizations that sponsor Group Relations conferences.

'Review' is usually for reflection on members' emerging *individual* conference experience – in particular the roles they have taken up in the conference. The focus is more 'internal'. 'Application Groups' – with a more 'external' focus – have been conducted in various ways, but almost always participants do pre-conference preparation about a work issue for exploration in the conference. The focus is usually on a 'problem' issue or an aspect of the member's work role.

The processes and models of application work have varied considerably. They have included presentation of the prepared issue to the group with peer feedback and input, assisted by a consultant. They have also included the application of various methodologies, such as 'Work Drawings', where members of the group represent their work experience graphically as a tool for projective exploration. In a recent conference with an 'A' and 'B' membership, the advanced group applied a version of Open Space Technology to develop key themes of interest, and worked in groups on selected themes.

Often these events initially focus on the way members take up conference roles which in application are related to work-place roles. Data has not been collected institutionally to assess the learning efficacy of different approaches. Instead the methodology is often selected primarily on the basis of individual preference or the past experience of an individual consultant. This points again to the relative absence of institutional learning – which may, however, occur informally.

Generally consultants to RAG groups are authorized to consult in ways they feel are useful. Participants have reported finding these groups very helpful in working on the conference experience and in providing new perspectives on their 'back-home' experience. The precise nature of this usefulness has not been documented nor formally examined in order to assess the particular methodologies that have contributed to learning. Instead, evaluation is generally based on informal feedback from members and on the consultants' informal evaluation. A useful way though that this has occurred with slightly more discipline is via the staff's dynamic exploration of the emergent RAG subsystem data. This approach lies at the heart of Group Relations methodologies – i.e. as a form of action research – and requires even more thorough consideration as a scientific methodology.

The extent to which the value of Review and Application as a learning method has been informally evident has resulted in my placing considerable emphasis on the RAG Event with increasing numbers of sessions allocated to this task. My colleague, Tania Nahum has been particularly instrumental in encouraging this and to giving greater consideration to post-conference application.

1.2. Follow-Up

In many of AISA's conferences, optional 'Follow-up Events' – half-day workshops that included Plenary and RAG Events – have been held between 4 and 6 weeks after the conference. They have tended to be a *continuation* of the conference experience rather than a more in-depth focus on application. Modest attendance at these events is a factor that has been insufficiently examined and may be another example of a missed opportunity for learning from conference experience.

In the design of the 2003 AISA national conference an optional – and different 'Follow-up Programme', 8 weeks post-conference was included, comprising either 6, 1½ hour weekly sessions, or 4 individual sessions with a consultant. Two consultants each ran these programmes, (which we thought of as 'Work Group programmes') and which were well attended and two consulted individually to members. Further exploration is needed to assess non-attendance. In some cases we knew that practical issues affected this. Informal feedback and the experiences of the staff indicated that the programme was very helpful to participants. This has encouraged me to include such a programme as a standard option in conferences, despite the evidence for its reported success not having been formalized. Subsequent requests for participants to complete a more formalized evaluation sheet produced only one response!

2. Learning for staff and sponsoring institutions

A major aspect of the primary task of AISA Group Relations conferences is the application of learning. In November 2002 a half-day event was held for past participants entitled *'What have we learnt from Group Relations work?'* Eighteen people attended – only a few of many hundreds who had attended conferences over the previous 16 years. The reasons for this poor attendance need to be considered.

The event began with a Plenary in which the conveners (me, Alastair Bain and Susan Long) and participants described some of our own learning. The contributions were rich. In three small groups we explored our individual experiences of application of learning.

In the final Plenary there was a report back and discussion. We learned, among other things, that:

- Group Relations thinking is experienced as a subversive activity – organizational application is difficult because of the way it challenges the current cultural norms. For a number of people the critical factor has been having a space with others who also understand or have been through a Group Relations experience. People felt alone with their learning after conferences. This was a valuable illumination of the difficulties of application. Many people felt isolated 'back home' through lack of engagement with like-minded people who had shared or who understood the experience and its value. While follow-up was useful, it did not really address the more pressing issues of maintaining, developing and applying longer-term learning. This suggests that useful post-conference application needs to be ongoing rather than one-off and needs to draw on peer support for its maintenance.

- There was a strongly expressed bid for a 'transitional space' to support people during post-conference adjustment, in working through the conference experience and in grappling with new workplace perspectives.

- The simplistic application of 'Group Relations methodology' without the broader context of conference-type experience was felt to be fruitless. The possibility of more than one participant from an organization might also be helpful in having a shared reality as well as in growing a critical mass of like-minded people in an organization. This points to the importance of offering more intensive links to members' organizations while also participating in a group of like-minded thinkers after the conference.

- The Group Relations conference has a *primary task of learning*. The workplace has its own primary task and even in an educational institution is unlikely to give organizational learning cultural predominance. To behave in an organization as if it is the same context as a Group Relations conference is incongruous and can impede the application of conference learning.

- There was a need to ensure that the learning from this exploratory event was applied to AISA itself and would be acted on by individuals in their AISA roles in ways that were useful for AISA and for future (and possibly past) conference participants.

This latter point leads me to consider the issue of learning for conference staff – at an individual level, but also at the level of sponsoring organizations. In this context I give consideration here to what I call 'applied' conferences, though all conferences might be 'applied.'

I have noted that the lack of formal assessment of and learning about the efficacy of Group Relations methodologies has been a limitation. The critical factor here is about learning at an *institutional* level. I have experienced and observed individual staff and conference directors implicitly and sometimes explicitly using action-learning methodologies to learn from conference experience for the development of Group Relations methodologies, and I will cite some examples. But I think we have failed to develop such processes systemically, to enhance institutional learning.

Similar examples of these processes occurred in two contexts. Firstly in taking up her Conference Director role, Susan Long introduced in AISA conferences a structure for staff to think about the data and to develop hypotheses about the Study Group systems. This involved an iterative process of organizing the data of the consulting experience into: major themes, transferences, counter-transferences and then hypotheses. Similarly, at the Leicester Conference in 2003, Mannie Sher provided a suggested framework for doing so. These approaches could be developed more substantially and applied in the context of broader systemic learning.

I am approaching other issues of staff and institutional learning in three ways: the development of staff; the processing of conference dynamics; and the application to sponsoring organizations. In some ways this parallels the learning of conference members: their own development; their learning from the emerging conference dynamics, and their application to their 'back home' organizations. I address the first two issues together as they are closely intertwined.

2.1. Pre-conference staff meetings and staff learning

For administrative and marketing purposes, but mostly for dynamic reasons, my staff meet up to 6 times before a conference and for a day just before the conference begins. Usually this has been by teleconference between Perth, Melbourne, Sydney, and also with UK and German-based staff members.

We collaborate from early on in conceptualizing, designing, managing and marketing the programme. This has been invaluable in part for the recruitment success of conferences, but more significantly in the contribution to a particular style of conference learning and working to which I am committed. It has also contributed significantly to supporting staff in their own learning and thinking about conference design, structure, process and management. Staff who have worked in other models have commented on the value of this approach. I note with interest that a requirement of the Tavistock when associated with the conferences of other organizations, is to participate in the design and planning.

2.2. Working with staff dynamics

In my leadership role, I place a premium on processing the dynamics of the staff group. Some view this as diluting the membership dynamics and depriving the membership of material that needs to be worked through by them. This has not been my experience. I believe that there is a reciprocal dynamic impact and exchange of relatedness and relationship between the staff group and the membership group. This is *the* data for us to work with. I think we need more systematically to attend to how this material might more formally operate as a medium for learning.

Susan Long once described one of the painful aspects of being a conference director as the discovery that the conference often organizes itself dynamically to mirror aspects of the director's internal world. I can wryly confirm this! I can also confirm the degree of learning this offers for members of staff. In addition to providing access to unconscious conference dynamics, it can also facilitate the work of the membership by not over-imposing *unprocessed* staff dynamics on the conference. Staff dynamics should not be *over-processed* either. By developing an understanding of staff dynamics, they can be worked with and worked from as critical data.

2.3. Organizational learning

In my recent staff roles in AISA, it has been difficult to pass on the learning from one conference to the next, especially when new staff are involved. AISA ran one, sometimes two major conferences each year for over 17 years, and several shorter group-relations based programmes. It was unusual for the same director to lead more than two consecutive programmes. Although occasionally conferences are either jointly sponsored or have co-directors or associate directors, for the most part there have been only Australia conference directors. Knowledge and learning about the history and processes of conferences and about taking up the role of conference director is thus restricted. A more explicit application of learning methodology – i.e. action-learning methodology – could support this.

2.3.1 Staff learning in the process of a conference
Conference Administration

When I was invited onto the staff and then to direct conferences, I became aware of two particular considerations: one to do with administrative process, the other to do with the evolution of learning. Regarding the former, sometimes because of lack of administrative continuity as well as the particular value placed on the role of Conference Administrator and, sometimes because of insufficient passing on of learning, each conference felt like it was 're-inventing the wheel' (as one Conference Administrator described it). I became aware of the importance of passing on knowledge and experience that could better prepare subsequent conference staff and directors. Sometimes this was at a quite concrete but dynamically significant level. An example of this was the inclusion in a brochure of an out-dated arrangement with a car-hire company to assist members to travel to the venue. Members' discovery that this information was invalid led not only to transport problems but also to the development of a view about the competence of the conference Management.

Administrator and Director as subsystem

Exploration of the dynamic experience of the Administrator, in role, as well as between Administrator and Director, has produced valuable learning about the dynamics of the conference institution. This phenomenon may also provide insight into the dynamics of the *sponsoring* institution, as these inevitably penetrate the conference. It has been suggested (Nahum, 2004, personal communication) that the dynamics of sponsoring institutions may – in parallel process – model (for better or for worse) organizational dynamics for conference members.

Boundary management

For example, for many years AISA's major conferences were held at the same venue in Lorne, a coastal village about 2 hours from Melbourne. The negotiation of a range of boundary issues with the venue often had to be repeated at each conference as though the venue and AISA representatives had forgotten the problems and solutions faced each year. One example was the different understanding of time boundaries that affected conference events when meals were not served on time.

Marketing

A more telling example was that the marketing and recruitment processes of each conference always seemed as though there had been no or little learning from the outcomes of previous marketing endeavours. While this inadequate passing on of learning was an administrative nuisance, inadequately repaired each time, the passing on of conference experience itself was a more dynamically significant issue.

Staff development and learning

When I took on the role of Director, I 'learnt on my feet'. I had the lucky foresight to appoint two very experienced past directors onto the staff, who proved to be enormously supportive and helpful during the conference experience. Of course this could have been a dynamic nightmare, but Alastair Bain and Susan Long acted with great generosity to me.

I have adopted a policy in my appointment of staff to always include a mix of experienced and relatively inexperienced members.

In addition to the fresh perspectives and often the challenge to established ways of working that newer people bring to the staff group, they and the sponsoring organization are also afforded the opportunity for learning about Group Relations consulting and conference management.

While I am referring here quite concretely to some of the structural considerations, I think that these operate in tandem with other sorts of learning. For example, I feel that the very challenging experience of discovering the role, tasks, authority and dynamics of conference directorship for neophyte directors (and equally for other staff roles) could be enhanced in other ways. I am also interested in how the experience and learning of a director could be passed on to future directors.

This is important for two reasons: firstly for the importance of preserving the concrete as well as the dynamic historic knowledge and secondly for the training of potential directors.

2.3.2. Learning methods outside the conference

Directors' Forum

The then AISA Executive supported me in the establishment of a 'Directors' Forum' for people who worked (and might work) in this role. The task was to share knowledge and experience; to explore issues of conference design; and to further our own development while keeping alive the learning from past and current programmes. While moderately useful, it tended to function as a consultative body making recommendations to the Executive about future programmes and the appointment of Programme Directors, diminishing its learning potential. A forum like this could develop the more formal action-learning process I have described above.

Staff Conference review meetings

I have introduced a post-conference review meeting. This has proved invaluable on two counts. Firstly, it fruitfully extended staff's post-hoc learning about some conference dynamics. Secondly it helped work through painful experiences with which some staff had been left. An example of the former related to the experience a staff member in an Associate Director role had of being obliterated in the closing plenary. This exploration led to a deep understanding about the dynamics of co-leadership. The value of this experience supports its continuation and development. Such learning about the relationship of the two roles could be fruitful for future staff.

Members' feedback

There has been a long-standing reluctance in AISA to obtaining formal feedback from members about their learning from conference experience. Might this interesting phenomenon mean that we could not bear to hear about conference learning experience that may not have been helpful? Or have we so idealized the model of learning that we are reluctant to look too closely at it or to recognize its limitations? This is a potentially valuable and fruitful learning opportunity for sponsoring organizations.

2.3.3. Hindrances to organizational learning

One element of this reluctance may emerge from the psychoanalytic stance from which we have drawn aspects of our staff roles. Elements of this are invaluable in taking up *consulting* roles in study groups and other events. But this useful stance in the consulting role may not apply to the *management* role. This is an important distinction. The sometimes-rigid way staff have taken up roles to deny this distinction and may be in some respects more appropriate to the psychoanalytic consulting room than to the conference management role.

Susan Long suggests that the 'after conference' application events that are successful are in part because of the new learning relations that are established between staff and participants – because of the very fact that people can start moving out of transferential relations and work more collaboratively. There is powerful learning from both styles – for different occasions and purposes.

She suggests that experiential learning is very powerful for the individual. Institutional learning occurs when there is movement at a broad collective level: not simply many insights for many individuals, but also a set of agreements between people. She sees organizations and institutions as fields of agreements and collusions. If the temporary institution learns, then it is not *sustainable* except as learning through the individuals – for the very fact that it is temporary. It gives members the recognition that group and institutional change is possible – perhaps in their more permanent groups and institutions. This was supported by the observations made at the event for conference participants described earlier.

I have written elsewhere about the relationship between the 'executive' and 'caring' functions with which managers who come from a clinical background struggle (Shafer, 2003). This struggle may apply to conference staff roles too because of the psychoanalytic origins of Group Relations work. This may also provide an inappropriate model of organizational functioning that constrains the picture of organizational management and leadership which members then are expected to apply to their work settings.

It might be hypothesized that Group Relations has swung so far away from forms of learning other than the experiential one within its own tradition, that it has become unable to learn through other methods and actively eschews them even when appropriate: an active split.

2.3.4. Learning Difficulties for sponsoring organizations

It has been striking how historically, Group Relations organizations are notoriously unable themselves to manage the kind of organizational dynamics we learn about in conferences. I have been curious about my own reluctance to say more about this because I feel that it would be washing AISA's dirty linen in public. This may be one of the contributing reasons to our limited capacity to apply our learning to our own organizations. It may be too painful. (With hindsight the demise of AISA in 2004 confirms this).

However there are some comments I can make that may contribute to this issue. AISA had recently undertaken changes to its organizational structure that have been both very painful and fruitful. One of these changes was the establishment of various Directorates. In particular the role of 'Director of Group Relations' (and other programmes) – to which I was appointed – is relevant here. This role had the authority for the development of Group Relations programmes over an extended period and for the appointment of programme directors.

Indeed the creation of this role may be, as Veronika Grueneisen has pointed out to me, one of the necessary presuppositions for organizational learning of the sponsoring organization (Grueneisen, 2003). She suggests 'Only if you in your role take an interest in what another director or administrator or staff does and can have them reflect on it with you (and other staff and directors included) will there be an interest in passing on. This organizational interest is embedded in your role. There is, of course, a difficulty in that every staff needs freedom to do what they think appropriate, but if they are authorized by you, then it appears to be appropriate to have them report back and reflect together and thereby contribute to the learning of the sponsoring organization.' This role carried with it the challenge of holding on to and learning from AISA's history while carefully thinking about future innovations so that past and present learning and different learning modalities could be valued but also challenged and developed.

In concluding, I want to refer to the theme of what was the next planned – the 17th – AISA national conference: 'Learning for Leadership: Flexibility, stability and the growth of new ideas'. (This conference never ran because of AISA's demise.) This theme not only parallels and reflects the organizational developments with which AISA was grappling, but also shows the challenges of organizational life today, and in particular those facing Group Relations. Reflections about this theme among the staff group of that conference, suggested that in engaging with new ideas, it needs to be recognized that there is unlikely even to be agreement about the stability of old ideas. Indeed, old ideas are not set in concrete, they are in constant evolution themselves, as well as in our perceptions of their past. It might further be considered whether the growth of new ideas may be anxiously associated with instability, rather than flexibility.

CHAPTER NINE

Applying Group Relations learning to the daily work of consultants and managers

Theorists solve the problems they want to; practitioners solve the problems they have to

Lilian Hupkens

Introduction

T his paper is based on original work done for the Belgirate Conference. 'Original' can be read in a double sense. Original because it was done firstly for the conference, and original because I decided to do completely new research as opposed to studying literature and writing a paper based on 'old' knowledge. For this research I decided to interview participants of past conferences, focusing on how managers and consultants in organizations apply their learning from Group Relations conferences in their daily work. This chapter describes the intensive interviews done as research and the results it led to. At the end of the chapter the results are compared with the literature in this field.

Background

The starting point for this work was a request from the organizers of the Belgirate Conference to give a presentation on the application of the learnings of Group Relations conferences in the business world. I decided to do new work that meant interviewing people active in the business world who had attended Group Relations conferences. My aim was to find out what their experiences had been like, what they had learnt there and how they applied this new knowledge in their daily work. The number of interviewees is relatively small, but I believe that the in-depth interviews and their analyses provide new observations and insights, and enrich knowledge regarding the application of the learning from Group Relations conferences.

Methodology and description of the research

The research group was made up of people in the Netherlands whom I knew had been to Group Relations conferences. I selected an equal number of men and women; from different backgrounds and professions who had been to conferences in Germany, France, the Netherlands, Spain and the United Kingdom. The fact that they had been to conferences in different countries organized by different Group Relations organizations could imply that the learning was not limited to one type of conference only, but could be generalized to Group Relations conferences in general.

The five interviewees were:

Mr. A was an education manager in a business school and had attended 1 conference as a member.

Ms. B worked as a management-recruiter and as consultant/trainer. She had attended 2 conferences as a member.

Ms. C was a consultant in the field of multiculturalism and diversity and had attended 6 conferences in 3 different countries as a member.

Mr. D was a business consultant; he had attended 4 conferences as a member in 2 countries and been on Staff twice as Administrator.

Ms. E had worked as a manager and as a management consultant; had attended 5 conferences in 3 countries as a member; had been on Staff twice as Administrator and twice as consultant.

Doing interviews, I found that interviewees had difficulty in discerning between the different conferences and tended to lump them together into one amalgam: 'Group Relations conference experience'. I therefore asked them first to go through their memories of conferences and put them in chronological order. When they had the dates and places in order I would go back and review each conference with them. What do you remember as being the most striking experiences there? For example what had been 'Ah-ha' experiences that had opened their eyes or hearts to certain phenomena. After going through the conferences in that way, I asked what they had learned in each conference, and how they applied the acquired knowledge in their daily work, if it had changed their way of working and their way of looking at various phenomena.

Whilst my initial question had been simply 'How did you apply the learning, particularly using concrete examples?' my focus changed and broadened. It became clear that I also had to pay attention both to what they had experienced there and also to the way they came to attend Group Relations conferences and what had been their motivation.

The interviews were very intensive because they started a whole train of thought and reflection in the interviewee, sometimes leading them to a completely new understanding of certain events and career changes. Several times I had to make more than one appointment because the interview led to so much thinking and remembering on the part of the interviewee that we were not able to finish in the two or three hours we had planned. During the interviews I made notes. After each interview, I wrote down my associations to that interview, what had been my own learning points from what I had learnt from my own conference experiences in order to make sure I could distinguish between what was 'theirs' and what was 'mine', to prevent contamination.

As all that material percolated in my mind, it resulted in a list of observations and conclusions not only regarding the applications of learning from Group Relations conferences, but also regarding the nature of the learning and the reasons leading people to attend Group Relations conferences. These findings are presented in chronological order: the process that people go through before, during and after a Group Relations conference.

Findings

The findings of the research were categorized under the following headings.

1. When and why do people attend Group Relations conferences?
2. What do they learn there?
3. How do they apply conference learning in their work?
4. How has conference experience changed their way of working?

When and why do people come to Group Relations conferences?

The first conclusion from this research was that the people who were interviewed did not go to a Group Relations conference 'out of the blue'. All of them had been in some kind of a developmental track or training program where at a certain point in time a Group Relations conference seemed useful or just the next logical step to take. Some had been in a personal developmental track where they had done a lot of reading on the subject, and/or were in psychoanalysis and a conference was just the next step along the path they were on at that moment. For others such a conference was part of a training course, a module, for a psychodynamic counselors' or a management trainers' training programme.

The conclusion I draw here is important for planners and designers of Group Relations conferences. The idea that a manager receives a conference brochure and thinks that it might be interesting, just as he might find a Business Unit Management course interesting, is entirely fictitious. It just doesn't happen that way. People need to be in a certain state of mind or development so that the ground has been prepared as it were, ripe for a seed to fall into.

Another observation was that in making the decision to attend a Group Relations conference it can be helpful if a colleague had previously attended, demonstrating that a conference is something one 'can do'. In one case an interviewee, who is a consultant, knew about Group Relations conferences from the literature, but only when he read an article in the Newsletter of the Netherlands Council for

Management Consultants did he realize that a Group Relations conference is not a 'touchy/feely', and he decided to attend.

In a second case, someone who knew me and read my name in a Leicester brochure, felt confident enough to go himself. Apparently there is a hurdle to take or a threshold people have to cross in order to decide to attend; and it seems that knowing others have been there is helpful to them.

A third observation was that people impressed by the experience of a Group Relations conference, then want to attend more Group Relations conferences. In the Netherlands people often choose to attend conferences in other countries. Some attended a few conferences in quick succession whilst others waited a few years, before deciding to attend again.

What do managers and consultants experience and learn there?

I asked the interviewees what kind of incidents had stuck in their minds. Most were able to answer that quite easily. But the question of the learning was more complicated. First thing, the conferences did not stick out separately in their minds or memories. They had fused into one amalgam, and it needed tracing back through time and noting down the years to be able to distinguish between them. Second thing, most of them did not only attend conferences, but also did a lot of reading or personal study in between or attended a training course. Therefore the learning was not confined to just the conference experience. It was more a swallow-tailing of theory into the practice of the conference. The one reinforced the other. For example Mr. C had read extensively about theories on groups and group processes. Also he was in psychoanalytic therapy. When he attended Group Relations conferences bits of the puzzle fell into place and he could explain certain phenomena because of his theoretical knowledge.

In the next paragraph I will describe some of the most striking experiences that my interviewees named. Those lists may seem limited on first reading. However when the interviewees later described how they applied the learning in their work, they came up with more extensive and varied descriptions compared to their initial memories. It would therefore seem that what people remember as being a striking experience or an important one does not necessarily determine their learning.

What kinds of experiences are particularly striking or memorable? Mr. A, who attended one conference, remembered in particular:

1. the Opening Plenary with a Staff who seemed so distant and 'hostile';
2. the Small Study Group with a non-responsive consultant;
3. the Large Study Group so cramped and unreal;
4. the aggressive emotions between two colleagues that had a paralyzing effect on the Small Study Group.

What had been strong feelings for him was 'déja vu' from the Sensitivity Trainings of the 1970s. It looked as if there was nothing new under the sun, but now the experience was from another experiential and professional viewpoint. What had also been strong was the amazement about human behavior, how programmed people are in certain situations.

Ms. B had attended 2 conferences and remembered:

1. a feeling of exhilaration in the large groups in both the Plenary and the Large Study Group, and she had felt free to speak her mind;
2. small groups seemed to pressure one individual into breaking down emotionally, without rules or intent;
3. the pressure of the group on the individual;
4. admiration for a consultant being able to pinpoint the issues in the Review and Application group.

Ms. C attended 6 conferences in 3 different countries. Some of these had been conferences based on the Harold Bridger model, a different kind of Group Relations-oriented conference. Her own opinion when she reviewed the conferences was that she was at a different point in time in each conference and learnt new things. She described her experiences as follows:

In the First conference:

- people becoming extremely angry during the Opening Plenary
- being able to be in contact with own feelings, putting action on hold

Second conference:

- noting gender differences, noting that men dared challenge boundaries
- trying out her own male part and thus playing with boundaries and taking up roles of authority

Third conference:

- the large study group 'managing oneself in role'
- the importance of own family dynamics
- it all looked familiar but it was still frightening.

After four conferences she felt she knew everything and went to one in another country and was amazed and surprised at how much there was still to learn. But during her sixth conference in a distant country, she noticed she had great difficulty and was very impatient with other participants for whom it was a first-time experience.

Mr. D had attended four conferences and had been administrator twice. He said that in the first conference he just tried to survive; in the second conference he began to understand some of the things and that in his third conference he felt that he could start applying some of the knowledge/experience and play or experiment with it. One of his most remarkable experiences had been the realization of how great the influence is of the group on the individual and that the individual takes on a role on the group's behalf. This had changed his view of seeing people only as individuals. He also remembered the overwhelming feeling of being in a large group of people. In his first conference the total membership was under 20. That, he learnt later, was a relatively small Large Group, but still the feeling of being overwhelmed was astounding. He also noted that as he attended more conferences there was a growing appreciation of the Staff's work in staying in role despite attacks on that role by members.

Ms. E. named as her most remarkable experiences:

- The realization that one can actually survive in a large group.
- Being given the time to think about stepping over the boundary into a conference, taking time to think about what she was feeling and being allowed to do so.
- The enormous regression that takes place in people in groups, making them dangerous and literally life-threatening.
- For the first time in her life actually feeling projected into, when she turned around to see who was being shouted at, because she couldn't imagine she was being shouted at.
- This experience led her to know that she could actually feel the difference between someone talking to her and someone projecting onto her. This was important for her because as an executive manager in an organization in the middle of organizational turmoil a lot does get projected onto authority figures.
- The importance of a structure in time, task, territory and someone to facilitate groups that have to work together. Also the realization that structure provides safety and protects people literally against themselves and their regressive tendencies.

When interviewing these people I noticed that in describing their experiences it seemed as if for each of them there had been some central and personal issue. Some had one central theme, which became more and more elaborated on in each conference. One interviewee had the issue of 'role' and how it affects people; another's issue was 'being different'.

My hypothesis prior to this research had been that the strongest emotional experiences generated the most learning. However, when it came to talking about the ways in which they applied their conference learning to their daily work, it turned out that the application was much more varied and broader than the themes or subjects that had struck them during the conferences. It could therefore be said that the learning was not directly linked to their strongest emotions during the conferences but that was much broader and had been acquired by osmosis as it were, during the whole conference.

How is the learning applied?

Two aspects came into the foreground: their way of looking and seeing had changed completely, and what we could call 'the observing ego' had been developed.

In general, the interviewees had found their way of looking at groups, their way of seeing things, had changed. It was as if they had acquired a new and different pair of spectacles to look through. Now, when they enter a room they are aware of where people sit, in which order the others enter a room, who is the first one to speak, etc., thus acquiring information about the group in a way that was new to them. They realized that this way of looking is not Extra Sensory Perception or clairvoyance, but that they could actually observe facts in reality, that have meaning, and were not simply random.

The observing ego was not named literally, but rather how it worked for them. One person said that at work, it seemed as if a tape recorder in his head kept up the observation and internal commentary. Another person described how he now could work at two levels. At one level he was interacting with the client about content, and on the other level he was in contact with the 'here and now'. He stated this gave him extra information about what was going on, and kept him from going along with fantasies and flights of the client.

Their 'observing egos', had been developed by their experiences in the here-and-now events of the conferences.

Taking an overview of all the different examples people gave of what they had learned and how they applied it, four main areas can be distinguished where they clearly see differences before and after attending conferences. These four main work areas are:

a. in their contacts with clients
b. in their contacts with a colleague
c. in their contacts with a group of people
d. in designing group activities such as working conferences, management retreats, sound boarding groups etc.

I will demonstrate the above by giving examples of what the interviewees said about how their way of working has been affected by their experiences.

In their contacts with clients

Ms. B now works as a counselor. She states that during intake with a client she now asks more about the context of work and/or family. Also she finds that she is able to explain about what happens in a system, what roles do they hold and how that operates in a system like the family or at work. In family therapy or mediation, seeing that system as part of a larger system helps her create a distance. She says she is less focused on 'personality', seeing people more as having different facets that come into view in certain settings.

Ms. C stated that in counseling future expatriates she now asks questions explicitly about person, role, organization in the country of residence. She talks about boundaries, contracts, the roles, gender, culture, age. She said she now also dares to make a prognosis and show where things could fail.

Mr. A, the business school education manager, said he now takes time to look more closely at reactions and interactions with people, trying to find the underlying message and being able to come into contact with that, to access it.

Mr. D, the management consultant, stated that when he works with individuals, he now stays away from therapy-like activities, sticking to the task of consultancy and not becoming more personal.

In their contacts with colleagues

Ms C. explained that now before embarking on new projects with other colleagues, she speaks explicitly about the contract with them, the roles and their other arrangements. She tries to think it through to see how it will work, trying to predict or project into the future what the consequences could be of those agreements. Furthermore, during the training course or conference she monitors to see if the arrangements and agreements about role etc are being upheld. She says she is more alert to what happens in these respects and intervenes or gives feedback more quickly.

In their contacts with groups

More than one interviewee stated that during an intake or initial interview with a group of people from the organization, they find that observing phenomena, seeing who is sitting where or who is the first to speak, gives them the first inkling of what kinds of dynamics are visible. This is described as having developed a sixth sense.

One consultant said that he now thinks hard before suggesting a group event or a conference. When proposing a conference, he pays more attention to designing it. He is quite explicit about what is the aim or task, what are the boundaries, how does he protect the boundaries and the safety of the participants, and how to stay within the agreed time boundaries. He is now much more aware of his own role in working with clients and sticking to that role.

Another interviewee stated the difference as now considering group dynamics instead of looking at a person as an individual; looking at a person in terms of role, and what that might say about the group or the phase the group is in.

One person said he was now more able to facilitate conflicts without being drawn into the conflict because he was more in contact with the hidden desires of the two fighting parties and their attempts to make him part of it.

Are there disadvantages in attending
Group Relations conferences?

While writing about the usefulness of attending Group Relations conferences a question comes to mind: are there no disadvantages in attending Group Relations conferences? My interviewees did name some disadvantages.

One disadvantage for people for whom this knowledge is relatively new is when they 'see things' they tend to speak out loud and point out their observation. Often this is not helpful at all, because at that moment they are not able to do anything about it and may not be in the position to do so either. This is what Freud described: you can only say those things to a patient that the relationship is strong enough to carry, to hold.

Another interviewee spoke about seeing more and more of the dynamics in the system, which made it impossible for her to stay in the system because it cost her too much energy. Now she has chosen to stay outside of systems and to work in a small group of psychologists as a therapist cum counselor.

Findings compared to the theory

In the literature, I found that little is said about who learns what. In one of the recent publications (Gold and Klein, 2004) where the authors reflect on Harold Bridger's work it is said that Harold Bridger's view was that although psychotherapists did learn from attending Group Relations conferences and could apply the learning in their daily work, managers did not. He found that it alienated them from their work and he therefore designed conferences where there was less focusing on the 'here and now' and more work on the stated task of the group. We must remember that Bridger made his observation in the 1950s.

The managers and consultants whom I interviewed for this project were adamant about what they had learned and how they applied it. Does this invalidate Bridger's views? Perhaps the consultants acted more like therapists than like managers in the 1950s; perhaps the consultants' learning supports Bridger's views. Nevertheless the interviewed managers were extremely interested in psychodynamic theory and had read about it extensively. I assume that managers nowadays have more knowledge about psychological processes and have been to so many kinds of training that they are better prepared to learn from Group Relations conferences, as well as apply their learning than managers of 40 or 50 years ago.

Summary and conclusions

New research was done to chart the way in which people from the business world, managers and consultants, learn from Group Relations conferences and how they apply that learning in their daily work life. A number of participants from past conferences agreed to participate in in-depth interviews where their whole conference history was reviewed, why they went to Group Relations conferences, what they experienced there, what they had learnt and how they applied that learning. The results can be summarized as follows:

- People decide to attend Group Relations conferences only if they have been in some kind of developmental track that prepares them for this experience or if friends, colleagues or acquaintances have attended.
- What people remember as being their most striking experiences there does not automatically lead to their largest learning.
- People name many learning points, more than and not strictly related to their most striking experience during the conferences.
- Managers and consultants describe many ways in which they apply their learning. This application takes place in their contacts with clients, in their contacts with colleagues, in their contacts with groups and when designing group activities.
- In the 1950s the distinguished Harold Bridger postulated that managers do not learn from Group Relations conferences. The findings from this research suggest that nowadays managers have more sophisticated knowledge about psychology than in the 1950s and can profit from participating in Group Relations conferences

To summarise, I believe that the people interviewed are representative of a very significant number of the participants of Group Relations conferences nowadays and may represent the learning from those conferences and its application.

Part V

Post-conference reflections

The hubbub of conference experiences and their derived meanings for individuals and systems, may be lived in the moment, but additional processing after the conference has ended plus contrasting with other conference experiences, expands thinking and adds to our knowledge.

Jan Baker and Joseph Triest have tackled different and similar aspects of Group Relations conferences. What they have in common is their attention to unconscious processes involved in learning that are profoundly influenced by Klein's and Bion's ideas of the 'container/contained'. The authors have used these ideas to deepen understanding of those factors that can limit or foster our knowledge that comes from the experience of exploration. The defences of the 'very small group' and the relevance of the 'system-in-the-mind' (Baker), the presence of 'autistic', 'homosexual' or 'heterosexual' patterns (Triest) in Group Relations conferences, broaden and deepen our knowledge of conferences and organisations and societies we work in and consult to.

They both describe the ubiquitous dramas and dilemmas that individuals and groups place themselves in and are placed in, to carry out unconscious functions, especially of the holding of 'otherness' that is a source of anxiety and is faced directly only with difficulty. The analysis of their experiences opens up insights for the reader into group phenomena from the psychoanalytic, systems and chaos theory perspectives. They describe the potential in groups for non-learning, be 'tempted to play out the familiar, take few risks and thus learn as little as possible' (Baker) or for evolving into 'close systems which do not allow an examination of ideas and thoughts' (Triest).

These two papers point to the persistent inhibitors of learning and to the desire, often observable in organisations, to have established practices confirmed, rather than to seek changes in contemporary paradigms and arguments to challenge them.

Baker's paper fosters the idea that creative thinking and knowledge in organisations can emerge in a Very Small Group, often on the boundary of the system, as a space for 'transformational thought and growth'. Triest's paper focuses on the link between the desire to know and the desire to establish relationships with others, how learning and knowledge can only ever be an outcome of relationships.

The authors of both papers use their conference experiences to challenge tendencies towards hiding from reality; to learn about our capacities for relatedness; to avoid 'aristocratic teaching'; and to face the encounter with 'otherness'.

CHAPTER TEN

The Very Small Group

Its role and function in the 'system in the mind'

Jan Baker

> The knowledge imposes a pattern, and falsifies,
> For the pattern is new in every moment
> And every moment is a new and shocking
> Valuation of all we have been.
>
> *East Coker*
> T. S. Eliot: *Collected Poems 1909–1962*

Introduction

The ideas in this chapter were stimulated by the Belgirate Conference (2003). It seeks to explore the meaning and function of the Very Small Group, a group with 3–5 members, whose existence, in my experience, is frequently established by members of Group Relations conferences in the Institutional Event, which 'focuses on the conference as an institution with its beliefs and ideas on the exercise of authority' ('Leicester' conference brochure, 2003). The VSG in the Institutional Event may mirror in size both the conference Directorate and the senior management groups of outside organisations. When such a group forms spontaneously in a Group Relations conference, it is often interpreted as setting up a rival alternative to the conference management and may indeed have similarities in both its structure and composition. This is then taken to be an envious attack by the membership, or 'acting out' of omnipotence or subversion.

Whilst this may be the case, I propose that there is also 'something else', something else to think about in relation to the creation of this group. What then needs to be explored is the 'system-in-the-mind' of the conference participants, including the management and consultants. Does this lead to meanings for the institution as a whole and, thus, outside institutions in the world 'back home', that would be worthwhile to consider? The hypothesis is that the 'system-in-the-mind' of the participants, a system of largely unconscious processes, seeks and finds those with a particular valency to be part of this intimate grouping because of the need to connect and in order to provide a vehicle for some change at the boundary to take place. This chapter examines this hypothesis, making use of Gosling's (1981) and Bion's (1963) notions of 'container/contained'. In order to do so, it develops the idea of the 'system-in-the-mind' and what it means to cross a boundary, which may itself provide the space for transformational thought and growth.

As case examples, the chapter takes two recent Group Relations conference experiences (Belgirate, 2003 and the Forum International de l'Innovation Sociale, [F.I.I.S.], Paris 2004), which both created a VSG in the Institutional Event. On both occasions these were composed of people whose history led them to position themselves on a boundary, which may then have given the opportunity to see things from a different perspective.

The Very Small Group (VSG): Some theoretical background

The VSG, whilst not always a formal part of the Group Relations conference structure, is used in some Group Relations conferences for 'B' members or for the Training Group (those more experienced participants who wish to develop their facilitative and consultative skills further) instead of the Small Study Group. Furthermore, the

VSG may be present in the Application Groups, but these are not 'here-and-now' events, and the size of the Application Groups may be appropriate as supervision groups for members of the Training Group. Nevertheless, a VSG was created spontaneously in both the conferences I am describing. Why then would such a group be created? The obvious advantages, as articulated by Gosling (1981) are that the VSG starts with a promise of safety and familiarity. By its very nature and size, this group will be able to work face-to-face and there will be fewer projective processes than present in a Small Study Group (approximately 12 members). So, it may have the function of re-creating a family-like form, and as such, a focus for the conference membership, of the exploration of wishes and fears: the wish for autonomy and the fear of aloneness, the wish for distance and the wish for, and fear of, intimacy.

Hirschhorn (1988) calls these groupings 'covert coalitions' which function as an organised form of basic assumption behaviour. He postulates that these relationships echo family life, but that people may take up roles which the group or system requires them to in order to control anxieties and which necessarily then provide inhibitions of sexuality and sexual tensions. Gosling (1981) also notes that what starts with a promise of safety becomes dangerous because of the awareness of the sexual nature of such a group, and the possibility of intimate pairings. This may make true learning (learning which incorporates emotional experience) difficult as there may be the temptation to play out the familiar, take few risks and thus learn as little as possible.

The VSG, of three people, recreates triangular relationships, which re-evoke Oedipal configurations and concomitant conflicts and anxieties. Britton (1992) writes that the depressive position (Klein, 1940) and Oedipus complex arise out of every life crisis or situation and need to be re-worked in each new life situation. This then is not a static situation, but a re-visiting and re-experiencing of these conflicts and difficulties so that, hopefully, life may be lived more thoughtfully and thus more fully.

So, it can be seen that the VSG offers a model of thinking about threesomes and of reworking Oedipal issues within a bounded space. This itself offers the exploration of a space, a potential or 'transitional' space (Winnicott, 1974) that is a forerunner of creativity and imaginative thinking. This then offers the space to 'play', as

Winnicott (1974) would see it, so that new patterns of imagining emerge and the world is continually created and re-created in the imagination (Davis and Wallbridge, 1981). There is, of course, the possibility that such creativity does not take place and Oedipal issues are not worked through to what may be called 'depressive position' thinking. If loss and mourning cannot be tolerated, nor the envy of the parental relationship, which is procreative while the parent–child relationship is not, then an Oedipal fantasy, according to Britton (1992) may develop instead. This is to deny the parental sexual relationship and create an Oedipal illusion, a defensive organisation where the parental relationship is known, but not acknowledged. Thus, he says, an Oedipal romance is created which is an organisation in rivalry to the parents' feeding and reproducing capacity, prompted by envy and knowledge of their creativity. The Oedipal illusion is a form of 'psychic retreat' (Steiner, 1993) where the pain of psychic reality is denied and there is a fantasy of remaining the 'chosen ones'. So, in summary, the VSG offers us both these possibilities, and perhaps moves between them in time and space. 'The 'system–in-the-mind' then, that this group represents on behalf of the conference membership is both created and longed for, yet can also become a psychic retreat or an illusional, and potentially destructive, place.

The 'container/contained' relationship

In order to develop my thinking about the role and function of the VSG, within the 'system-in-the-mind', I now move on to a description and discussion of the 'container/contained' relationship (Bion, 1963). The prototype for the 'container/contained relationship' is the mother's breast/infant (Symington & Symington, 1996). Bion himself describes the idea for use as a model in which the 'container' can be receptive to the experiences of the 'contained', for example, what a mother does when she is receptive to her baby's stress and panic. If she is able to act as a container she will take in the baby's feelings, modify them through her own capacity for empathy and reflection, and then transform them into something that enables her to ease her baby's distress. It can be seen that the concept of

containment is an extension of what Klein originally termed 'projective identification' (Klein, 1946a) that is, ways in which a patient can
get the analyst to feel feelings and experiences that he cannot contain within himself and cannot express other than by getting the
analyst to feel them too (Bott Spillius, 1992). Bion extended the concept by making a distinction between normal and pathological projective identification and makes projective identification a more
active process on behalf of the mother (container) in relation to the
infant (the contained). He then took this formulation into a more
abstract realm where the container (a pre conception) searches for
and mates with a particular idea which then creates meaning. In
Bion's formulation this is a process for thinking: discovering and
developing thoughts within a bounded setting. This has been my
experience in the Institutional Event of a conference, for example
where meaning can be found (contained), and in this sense it may be
that the VSG attempts to carry out this search for meaning by offering itself and being offered to the conference structure.

'System-in-the-mind'

The second concept that I wish to present is the 'system-in-the-
mind'. Staff at the Grubb Institute first developed the concept of
the 'organisation-in-the-mind' (Hutton et al, 1997) or 'institution-in-
the mind' (Armstrong, 1998) as a way of thinking about what kind of
organisation was carried in the minds of the participants. This is the
perception individuals have of how the organisation is structured
and how activities and relationships develop. What are the pictures,
images and fantasies each member carries of the organisation? What
is allowed to be known to, and what has to be hidden from, consciousness? Hutton (1997) postulates the 'organisation-in-the-mind'
as a form of 'transitional object' (Winnicott, 1974) created yet also
discovered, unexpected and surprising, providing a link between
what is 'me', what 'not-me'. I prefer the notion of the 'system-in-the-
mind', where system is defined (*The New Oxford Dictionary of
English*, 1998) as 'a set of connected things or parts forming a complex whole: parts of a mechanism or an interconnecting network
. . .'. In my mind this makes an associative link with systems theory

with its attention to task, roles and functions and boundaries, and with other systemic functionings, for example the bodily system, computing systems or political systems.

The 'system-in-the-mind' provides a link between each person's view of the whole structure, be it an actual organisation or Group Relations conference. This is the map from which each person is working, but it is a map affected by individual thoughts and wishes, past history and experiences brought to the system. It may include what members want to believe is happening, what they want the management to believe is happening and what the management wants the members to believe is happening. When there is a flow of interaction then there may be positive experiences akin to Balint's 'harmonious, interpenetrating mix-up' (Balint, 1968), his phrase to describe the experience of the environment and the individual pene-trating one another, similar, in some ways, to Bion's 'container/ contained' model. This may be the interpenetration of the realms of emotion or the unconscious, or the realms of power and politics. It is the capacity to hold multiple perspectives, which Hatch (1997) has defined by using a 'collage' metaphor:

> When you use collage as a metaphor for organisational theory you are recognising the value of holding multiple perspectives and using parts of theories to form new work worthy of display in its own right . . .
>
> (Hatch, 1997: 54)

This requires the concept of mental space, a place where thoughts can be thought whilst resisting clinging to what is already known and it is in this space where we can tolerate what Bion called 'nega-tive capability' (quoting Keats): '. . . that is, where a man is capable of being in uncertainties, mysteries, doubts, without any irritable reaching after fact and reason' (Bion, 1970: 125).

Adopting this capacity for thinking may require the adoption of the 'stranger' or outsider position, either as an individual or in a small group setting. Both through the individual's valency for this behaviour, and the 'role suction' (Krantz & Gilmore, 1990) of the group, groups can exert pressure on the individual or small group to take up and enact this role on their behalf. It is as if the 'system-in-the-mind' requires certain individuals to occupy this role for a transitional space to be created. So, by placing itself temporarily outside the system, the group may refuse to take the known world for granted and may not be prepared to adopt the 'thinking as usual' (Schuetz, 1944), but also can become marginalised or excluded. However, it may be that it is the very place, on the margins or boundary, that learning from experience can be acquired.

So far, I have written only of the possibility for real connectedness through the capacity to think from a boundary position. Another way of thinking about these phenomena is that the VSG of the type I have been involved in, through a process of projective identification, takes up a scapegoat role, providing something for the system-as-a-whole to attack or denigrate, or try to leave outside the system, because it is too frightening to think about. This then gives information about the system's unconscious functioning and basic assumptions behaviour, as different members or a group of members may be selected as targets for different aspects of the system's malfunctioning (Krantz & Gilmore, 1990). A further possibility is that the VSG may be constructed in 'the system-in the- mind' as a non-group, taking up a position which Lawrence, Bain and Gould (1996) called basic assumption 'me-ness'. This occurs when those meeting make a tacit, unconscious assumption that the group is to be a non-group, because the idea of being a group is too persecutory. Then people behave as if the group has no reality and the nature of transactions is inauthentic or instrumental with no place for feelings, desire or wish for change. In such a group there is little place for authority, differentiation of roles and tasks, and a 'pseudo-democratic egalitarianism' (ibid, 43) rules. It may be that the VSG could be pushed into taking up this position unconsciously in order to protect the rest of the system's functioning. Belonging and connectedness then can be seen to reside in the rest of the organisation in the 'system-in-the-mind', the VSG unwittingly providing a sacrifice to ensure the continuation of the wider system.

In this way of thinking, there is an 'either/or' solution: either work group functioning where the VSG acts as a conduit for communication, or basic assumption functioning, so that no transformation of the system takes place. However, Stacey (2001) suggests that desirable dynamics can be created by both work group and basic assumption functioning. Rather than positing either/or systems of stability (functioning) or instability (non-functioning) he proposes the idea of the need for 'bounded instability' between a work group (with basic assumption behaviour in the background) and a more prominent basic assumption group. It is this very place on the margin, or anxious edge, Stacey argues, that is the place of transformation. This is a place that is stable enough not to fall apart but unstable enough not to be stuck in one pattern of behaviour. It is from this position, where no one yet knows the outcome, that each person takes into account the responses of others and can 'play' creatively (Winnicott, 1974).

Case examples

I now come to two case examples, which I hope will illuminate what I have been writing about and extend our thinking of the role and function of the VSG. The first example took place in the Belgirate Conference, November 2003. As well as discussing the structure of the Group Relations conference, the various groups and events, we explored experientially the impact of various identity-related variables, such as nationality, professionalism, religion, geography, gender and race in relation to taking up roles in Group Relations conferences, and then what this might mean for our 'outside' work in organisations.

When the conference divided into these groups (nationality, professionalism, religion, geography, gender, race and others), there was initially a large group of members who designated themselves the 'Undifferentiated Other'. Initially this group concentrated on getting data from one another and other groups, but soon divided itself into three, with a small group of four persons. This small group was composed of two women and two men, similar in composition to the Directorate, of two male directors and two women administrators. In this VSG there was a woman from the UK (myself), a man from Israel, a Dutch woman and a Swedish man. Organizations represented, or represented in the mind, were OPUS (UK), OFEK (Israel), IFSI (France), AGSLO (Sweden). It was quickly established that we were able to work speedily and intensely with one another, and, as Gosling writes, formed intimate attachments.

We named the group 'Money, Politics and Power' and focused

specifically on the possibilities of corruption in relation to these areas in Group Relations conferences. Clearly, and perhaps in a rather grandiose and all-encompassing way, we were trying to address major themes, both of the conference and of outside organisational life. We thought about the 'currency' of the Group Relations conferences: not just the actual cost in monetary terms, but also the status of being chosen or being asked to contribute papers or expertise. Money has an obvious relationship to power, as it can pose a barrier to the entry of newcomers into a system.

It is evident that issues in relation to power are central in organisational thinking and occupy a key place in the 'system-in-the-mind'. As already discussed, power, Oedipal issues and desire are intimately related, and although in this VSG we spent some time discussing these intellectually, we did not mention sex. Why not? As already mentioned above and as Gosling suggests, the VSG becomes dangerous because of its intimacy, with the fear that what can be imagined may be made real, thus confusing and acting out Oedipal fantasies. So, we discussed money, politics and power in relation to what kind of system we were in. How did this system and its management make choices and decisions, select members for specific tasks or promote learning? How did it use its resources? Were these decisions based on the wish of the majority or did some members have higher status than others? What were the issues concerning rivalry and competition? How did the organisation link with other, similar organisations and on what basis? In this VSG we spent a lot of time meeting and discussing with other groups and management to try to understand and explore these questions further. What we thought less about, and this links both to the 'container/contained' model and the 'system-in-the-mind', is what we were playing out, not just for ourselves as individuals within this small group, but also for the system as a whole.

What I became more aware of, as I reflected on these events after the Belgirate Conference was over, were the boundary issues within the group, and the place each of us had occupied as a member on a boundary, or as a 'stranger' in relation to a group. Each of us had been born in one place and raised in another, each of us spoke two languages or more, each of us had found or felt ourselves to be in a sort of 'no man's land' at some stage in our lives. So what did it mean to place us together? As well as many other possibilities, (and we could discuss whether we were a work group or a basic assumption group or, as I think, both, at different times) I think we were placed in the 'stranger' position in order to open up this area for thought, that is, to examine and to challenge the 'thinking as usual', and to be able, as a whole system, to conceptualise something new and creative in relation to the task. The fact that we all spoke two languages or more also gave us greater possibilities and opportunities for communication across boundaries, and also for voicing some of the 'unspeakable' issues or some organisational taboos (such as money and power). Perhaps the VSG gave us as a group the necessary or the needed safety and protection to take up this difficult role in the system. I hypothesise that it was also a place where 'bounded instability' (Stacey, 2001) was located by the system. It was a place where some difficult organisational issues could be addressed and transformed through being more openly expressed, because it was a place of 'not-knowing', and because of the intensity of the desire to work creatively together.

My second example comes from the F.I.I.S. Conference held in Paris in March 2004. The VSG (of which I was a member again, wishing to expand what I had learnt in Belgirate) initially had three members, then four, then three again, and was formed during the Institutional Event. Taking my cue from the Belgirate Conference, this group was named 'something else'. Initially this group was composed of British (UK), American and Catalán (Spanish) members. Later the American woman left because she became too distressed by the projections from the whole system. Again, we could explore the various Oedipal issues and configurations, and certainly the challenge to the Directorate, with a similar membership of Catalán, Catalán-French and American (whose home is in England).

However, the most striking thing I want to relate is the feelings engendered by this group within the whole system and engendered in us. In relation to the 'container/contained' model and projective identification, I think we took up roles pushed into us by the whole system (playing out issues for the 'system-in-the-mind') in a form of 'role suction', to which our personal valencies connected. Once more, this group became very intimate and intense. This time sexual issues were apparent and, although not openly discussed, at least more available for thought. What was striking, however, was that no one wanted to join this VSG, even though the other groups were in

THE VERY SMALL GROUP   163

flux. At first we remained in splendid isolation and perhaps in a form of 'psychic retreat' where we played out 'Me-ness' and rather omnipotent feelings. However, we soon realised the need to connect with other groups, and invited others to join this VSG, which perhaps felt increasingly dangerous, and in danger of being isolated or excluded from the mainstream. On a visit to management, we were confronted by the Director asking, 'Are you members?' This had a profound and shocking impact. What position in the mind were we in, for ourselves, for the Management and for the 'system-as-a–whole'? If not members, then what?

Again we were occupying a boundary position and one where the American member felt increasingly disturbed. At this point we asked for some consultation, and received the interpretation, which was blindingly obvious but as yet unknown to us (Bollas, 1987). We were reminded of the composition of our group in relation to what was happening in the world outside; namely that we were a British person, an American, and Catalán Spanish. The war was still raging in Iraq, the position of the British and Americans hated and feared in equal measure, and widely condemned by most members of the conference. The Madrid bombings had taken place only two weeks before and there was also perhaps the associative link in the 'system-in-the-mind' (although not reality based) between a Catalán (strongly nationalistic) and the nationalistic and separatist Basque terrorist movement (ETA). No wonder no one wanted to join us, as we represented for the system all that was frightening and terrible, dangerous, a kind of 'nameless dread' (Bion, 1963). No wonder one member was at breaking point, although she saved herself by leaving the group and finding a more appropriate home. The only other member to join us was another Catalán who helped us to connect more appropriately with the rest of the system. In this example, the group was placed in this position perhaps both to keep the rest of the membership out of danger and away from explosive and annihilating attacks present in the mind, and for something terrifying and destructive to be able to be thought about within a bounded space.

Concluding thoughts

This chapter has attempted to explore the meaning of the VSG, frequently created spontaneously in Group Relations events. In doing
so it has explored two key, connected concepts: that of Bion's formulation of 'container/contained' and the idea of the 'system-in-the-
mind' which, I have argued, seek to provide containment for its
membership. In so doing, those who occupy a position on the
boundary may coalesce on behalf of the system into a VSG that then
holds something important for the system which, for healthy functioning, needs to be understood and addressed. For example, the
'unthought known', that is thought but not yet mentally processed
and thus put into words, may be explored more easily in this type of
VSG on behalf of the system. What, then, do these thoughts and case
examples offer us in relation to the theory and design of the Group
Relations conference and its application to the world of work? One
question is: may it be helpful to reinstate the VSG as a conference
event more often and in a different way? Would this enable us to
examine some of the issues explored in this chapter more exhaust-
ively, so that what is in the shadows can be examined more clearly in
the light, as we then have the apparatus to do so more easily? Whilst
this may be interesting to consider, I think that probably it would be
confusing the structure with what are necessary and meaningful
conference dynamics; in other words, that the meaning of the VSG
lies in the way it is spontaneously created. What we need to ensure
is that Group Relations conferences, whilst retaining the desire to
examine and explore organisations and the 'system in the mind'
do not become trapped by their own construct, images and ways of
thinking.

    As in the allegory of 'Plato's cave' (Morgan, 1986), we can choose
to stay in the shadowy world of appearances and what we think we
know, or take the risk to explore the world outside, not in the spirit
of finding utopia, but simply to learn more about our capacity for
connectedness and relatedness. The case examples in this chapter
illustrate the importance of this connectedness and relatedness and
the need for them to be acknowledged so as to promote creativity
and avoid splitting or denying the shadow parts of groups and systems. Therefore we may find ourselves in a space for thinking, a
'transitional' space, 'on the edge', where thoughts can be allowed to

run free. Taking this risk, the risk of 'not-knowing', I think is at the heart of the purpose and method of the Group Relations conference and one that can be further expanded and explored through opportunities offered us, as in the Belgirate Conference and in our institutions back home.

CHAPTER ELEVEN

In favor of reinventing the wheel

Reflections on the Group Relations model following the first Belgirate Conference

Joseph Triest

There is a popular Jewish tale about a poor Hassid whose name was, shall we say, Mendel, who had lived all his life in the small township of Yehupetz[1] and who one night had a dream. In his dream he saw a remote small township thousands of miles away, where a treasure awaited him – unimaginable wealth that was buried under the house of another Hassid, who lived there. Without further ado he prepared his bag and walking stick, made his farewells to his children and his wife – she must have thought, and probably not for the first time, that he had lost his mind – and went away. He travelled days, weeks, years, until he reached his destination; and to his great amazement, he found the alley, the house and the Hassid – his own spitting image! – just as he had seen them in his dream. With great excitement he told his story to the man; but the man's reply was far from enthusiastic: 'Fool', he said dismissively, 'do you not know that dreams are but false tellers? I, too, dreamed years ago that in Yehupetz lived a Hassid named Mendel, under whose bed a treasure was buried ... Much good

[1] Where live all the Jews with little money to spend, but big lessons to teach; wait and see ...

did it do me!'. So our Hassid hurried back to Yehupetz and in spite of his children's protest and against his wife's better judgment (whose complaints this time must have reached the highest spheres), he started to dig under his own bed and, sure enough, found the treasure that had been awaiting him there.

Could our Hassid from Yehupetz, the hero of this story, have found the treasure had he not set out on his treacherous and seemingly preposterous quest? Moreover, had he not met his like in the end of that journey, a twin in his own image who served him as a mirror and gave him what had been his from the start, would he ever have come to know the true value and real nature of his assets?

Following the Belgirate Conference, I chose to use this Hassidic tale in a way it was probably never meant, to discuss epistemic learning models in the context of the development of scientific paradigms. For the Belgirate Conference, too, was dreamt by two 'Hassids' – Mannie Sher, Director of the Group Relations Programme at the Tavistock Institute, and Dr. Avi Nutkevitch, then Chairperson of OFEK – who each set out on a journey, one from the township of Tel Aviv and the other from that of London, met half-way by Lake Maggiore, with an objective in mind to evaluate a 'treasure': the Group Relations model identified with the work of Eric Miller and A. K. Rice.

The more general question underlying this discussion is in fact posed by two disciplines studying the development of scientific models, namely, the philosophy of science and the history of ideas; how are scientific models established? How do they gain their impact? How do they become, how are they validated or refuted, and finally, how do they expire and give birth to new models?

It was Kuhn (1962) who suggested that 'normal science' develops not in a linear progression but through revolutions and reorganization; scientific paradigms, he claims, receive weight or expire not because of their internal contradictions[2] but, rather, in accordance with the processes within the scientific communities in holding them.

The term *paradigm* as used by Kuhn, stands for the entire constellation of beliefs, values, techniques, and so on, shared by members

---

[2] Contradictions are not only inevitable but, indeed, are an integral part of the process of scientific inquiry, used to explore the currently prevalent paradigm.

of a given community at a given time (Kuhn, 1962, p. 175). Kuhn's main point is that 'normal science' does not necessarily validate knowledge with direct relation to the paradigm's truth value. Actually, he states that choosing between competing paradigms is much like choosing between competing political institutions; it means choosing between mutually exclusive aspects of the community's life. Such a decision is inevitably dependent on the paradigms being evaluated, thus creating a self-confirming and circular process; each group uses its own paradigm to generate arguments in support of it. In order to find out how paradigms really change (or, using Kuhn's words, how scientific revolutions occur) we must explore not only the influence of nature and logic, but also the techniques of argumentation and persuasion used by the different groups in the scientific community (ibid).

What is true for paradigms in the natural sciences must be doubly true for paradigms dealing with dynamic psychological processes in and between groups – not to mention groups of 'scientists' (or professionals) whose common denominator is a paradigm about Group Relations.

Kuhn's thesis lacks from the start the tools that could lead it beyond the sociological dimension of the process through which science develops. This is why Kuhn cannot explain the appeal a given group of ideas has in a given community at a given time. To us, however, this could be an issue of cardinal importance: what is it that drives a group of scientists, researchers or professionals (ourselves, in this case) to develop and adopt a certain paradigm in a certain scientific, social and cultural context and to reject or ignore others? How does this community examine its own tools, and to what extent is it willing to tolerate information that threatens its basic beliefs?

It seems safe enough to maintain that the history of ideas (and even more so in Kuhn's version) might be enriched by some of Freud's, Klein's and Bion's contributions to the understanding of unconscious aspects of learning processes. The Group Relations model, particularly, has a lot to offer in this area. Indeed, this model, which integrates psychoanalytic approaches with notions taken from the theory of open systems, could shed some light on the conscious and unconscious dynamic forces that influence the creation and extinction of Kuhn's 'scientific establishments' and on the relations between a given setting of inquiry and the inner learning processes taking place in that setting.

On the relation between the desire to know, the capacity to think and early object relations

The truth is that this subject – i.e., the deep inherent unconscious link between interpersonal processes and thought, between the desire to know and the desire to establish a relationship with others – did not wait for Klein, or Bion or even Freud to be revealed. Indeed, it can already be found in the Old Testament, in the dual meaning, in the original Hebrew text, of the verb 'to know'. In Genesis 4:1 we read 'And Adam knew Eve his wife; and she conceived, and bare Cain . . .'[3]. In biblical Hebrew 'to know' had a sexual meaning, which in fact also exists, as a secondary and slightly archaic expression, in modern Hebrew. In this sense, we might say that Freud's psychoanalysis adopted the biblical understanding (although Freud preferred to refer himself to Plato's Banquet); by defining the subject through unconscious sexuality it bases knowledge of the self on a dialectic link to the other. In order to know myself (as a subject who is, by definition, only partly self conscious) I am doomed to rely on the help of another. The prism of sexuality (Eros) endows this other – the object of my desire – with a gender dimension and instates it as *different* and *complementary*. But from now on the subject must ask: what is it that I seek in the other in my efforts to know myself (through him or her); do I seek (in the object) that which is like me (the homosexual, narcissistic aspect of relationship) or that which is different from me (the heterosexual-complementary aspect of relationship)?[4]

In either case, it is the subject's need of the object in that role that creates the dialectic basis of 'object relations'. Without the other who serves as a mirror to me I cannot know who I am (where 'I' naturally

[3] Genesis, 4:1, King James Version. Interestingly, more recent and rather widespread translations omit the dual meaning; the same verset in the New International Version reads: 'Adam lay with his wife Eve, and she became pregnant and gave birth to Cain'.
[4] In this presentation of things, it goes without saying that no value judgment is associated with the use of terms such as 'narcissism' or 'homosexuality'.

includes those parts of myself that are unconscious). But there's a catch; once the definition of my identity is in the hands of the other (a 'not me' that is inherently different from 'me'), it can no longer describe me as I 'really' am, it can no longer represent my internally defined 'real self', as some spontaneous spring from within (Winnicott, 1960). The dialectic relation is therefore inevitable. Forever, I shall have to attempt to free myself from that other on whose recognition of my separateness and independence of him or her, I depend (Benjamin, 1990, quoting Hegel's 'master-slave' paradox).

The origin of the desire for knowledge therefore lies in a self knowledge that is based on knowledge of the other. But wanting to *know* is not the same as wanting to *learn*. In fact, in order to be able to learn you have to be able to admit *not-knowing*, which inevitably creates anxiety and frustration.

It seems that Freud (1911) was the first to point at that link between mental representation of reality (namely, thinking and learning) and object relations in a psychoanalytical context. He describes the state in which the gradually developing dominance of the 'reality principle' over the 'pleasure principle', is synchronous with the development of an ability to think and thus to bridge the gulf of frustration between the moment when a want is felt (the desire for the breast which is at first hallucinated) and the moment when action appropriate to satisfying the want is taken (namely, finding the breast in reality). A capacity to tolerate frustration thus enables the psyche to develop thought as a means by which the frustration itself is made more tolerable.

Klein (1930), following Freud, stresses the role of aggression in early object-relations, and directly links the capacity for primary symbolization – which is a necessary though not sufficient condition for any thought – to the infant's ability to tolerate anxiety and frustration. She relates primary learning processes to the infant's knowledge of the body – that is to say, the mother's body. The baby's unconscious fantasy about attacking the mother's breast (which represents the first external object) creates an unconscious and inevitable anxiety, which will drive the infant to defend itself by creating a symbol of the external object and through it of reality.

I shall now try to converge these ideas in order to propose three types of learning that are based on patterns of object relations. More specifically, I shall propose two kinds of learning based on the capacity to tolerate frustration and anxiety, and one type of non-learning resulting from the inability to tolerate frustration and anxiety. I shall refer to these types, respectively, as the 'homosexual', the 'heterosexual' and the 'autistic' paradigms.

The last will be discussed first, as it is in fact an exception, in that it is a paradigm aimed at blocking possible learning.

The autistic pattern

This pattern's sole purpose is to prevent the exploration and examination of ideas in reality. I'll quote Bion again: 'If intolerance of frustration is dominant, steps are taken to evade perception of the realization by destructive attacks. In so far as space and time are perceived as identical with a bad object that is destroyed, that is to say a no-breast, the realization that should be mated with the preconception is not available to complete the conditions necessary for the formation of a conception. The dominance of projective identification confuses the distinction between the self and the external object. This contributes to the absence of any perception of two-ness, since such awareness depends on the recognition of a distinction between subject and object. Inability to tolerate frustration can (thus) obstruct the development of thoughts and the capacity to think, though a capacity to think would diminish the sense of frustration intrinsic to appreciation of the gap between a wish and its fulfilment' (ibid).

The autistic pattern is therefore a closed system, protected against refuting, which does not allow an examination in reality of ideas and thoughts, does not allow learning from experience and is entirely mobilized to prevent links and to destroy object relations as such, in order to preserve internal coherence. But, paradoxically, the attempt to thus preserve coherence only results in exacerbating internal chaos.

Things are very different with the two other types of organization, or, more precisely, the two other dynamic aspects that accompany, to a varying degree, all learning, exploration or validation processes.

The homosexual pattern

The homosexual pattern is based on seeking in the other that which is similar, like-minded, confirming, approving. A good example is religious teaching not aiming to refute or question the knowledge already held by the learner, but, on the contrary, to confirm it. Is this futile learning? Not necessarily, as we see in the tale brought in at the beginning of this paper. Such learning is intended to allow the thinker to acquire a sense of value to his own thinking without threatening the foundation of his faith. It is intended to seek additional confirmation of existing assumptions. It does not ignore contradicting arguments but is mobilized to refute such arguments. Of note is the fact that Kuhn sees this as one of the characteristics of 'normal science'.

Its danger clearly lies in such fusion of ideas that prevents any new ideas from seeping through, and, more importantly, precludes any possible refuting of existing attitudes, even when these fail all possible reality tests. When the need to confirm that which already exists is stronger than the willingness to examine it in view of contradictory findings, there is permanent danger of creating a self-confirming closed system (a paranoid system in that it cannot be refuted). In such conditions a collapse into an autistic structure becomes possible.[5]

The heterosexual pattern

The heterosexual pattern, from the start, seeks that which is different; the learner wishes to explore new ideas, his desire is for the other, for that which is complementary. In such conditions, when an idea meets another, that is, a different idea, a new idea may be born which is integrative and creative (just as a baby is born out of an encounter between man and woman). However, as in any oedipal relationship, the competition between old and new ideas is in that case inevitable; in fact, in the heterosexual pattern there is no way to

[5] The paranoid system differs from the autistic position in that it acknowledges the existence of the other, even if it sees that other as a 'bad object'. Autism denies the existence of the object.

prevent new ideas from destroying and eventually replacing old ones. When this process takes place precociously, that is to say, before the theoretical model managed to become established, it could extinguish valuable existing knowledge before that knowledge could be fully extracted and receive its proper meaning. Such conditions, when models are destroyed before they have had the time to become established, resemble a quick collapse of a political regime which leads to anarchy.

In summary we can say, that in every process of establishing a model or a theoretical paradigm, both aspects – the homosexual and the heterosexual – must co-exist and must be balanced. The relative 'dosage' and timing are therefore critical factors in any learning process.

I shall now try to briefly outline the context on which the above thoughts have emerged.

The Belgirate Conference

The question that is at the heart of the discussion is this: what mutual influences can be found between the learning processes and the psychodynamic processes that take place in a given setting – that of a self-exploration of a paradigm with its own tools?

It was clear from the start that the Belgirate Conference – presented to participants as a re-evaluation and re-examination of the Group Relations model in light of current perspectives – was born under the sign of twinship: two founders, both of them men, both of them identified as Jews, both of them the respective leaders of organizations in whose founding Eric Miller was involved, with both organizations basically designed to offer sponsorship and an aegis to conferences organized according to the Leicester Model; OFEK in Israel and Tavistock in London.

A quick examination of the structure of the Belgirate Conference immediately reveals that those invited had already worked as consultants in conference teams based on the Group Relations model. Past conference participants who had not been privileged enough to be on staff were not invited, nor were any consultants who are working according to different models, or, for that matter, the general public. This deliberate homogeneity of the participants, which stands in contradiction with our usual tendency to create in our experiential conferences a human texture that is as heterogeneous as possible, inevitably gave rise to the suspicion that only the converted had been invited, as if to make sure that the examination would be kept 'in the family'. Or, as one participant put it: 'it seems that the cardinals of the Tavistock church feared that an overly exposed examination of our secret religion in the presence of non-believers could bring down its foundations'.

Could this indicate an unconscious anxiety that accompanied the conference from the start? Could the invitation to re-examine a model whose originators are Eric Miller and A. K. Rice be not just an 'academic matter', but also include in its unconscious shadows a hidden challenging of the Founding Fathers, as well as an attempt to 'win the crown' (the model's crown of epistemic authority)? Could that have been the opening of a succession struggle between the 'sons' (Mannie Sher, Avi Nutkevitch) and other male or female pretenders (e.g., the two keynote speakers, Olya Khaleelee, the late Eric Miller's wife, and Mira Erlich-Ginor, the former President of OFEK) to the same throne?

I wish to further develop this idea about the nature of the anxiety aroused by the conference's Primary Task, and the way it was expressed in the structure and dynamics of the exploration process that evolved during the work. I shall do this by analysing certain events that took place within an experiential session led by the organizers.

In the said session participants were invited to freely divide into groups based on several possible criteria pre-set by the design of the event. The purpose of the exercise was to investigate how different identity parameters affected role taking in conferences. The pre-set identity parameters were gender, race, religion, nationality, profession and 'other'.

The task definition emphasized that each group should examine the parameters around which it was organized. Inter-group meetings were allowed but limited to the discussion of the specific perspective initially chosen by the group. This phrasing of the instructions was perceived as somewhat restrictive, probably because it might have been expected that the invitation for participants would be so formulated as to allow each group to explore the whole system as it saw it. As early as in that first stage it already seemed that the definition of the event's Primary Task, too, had been impregnated with

that unconscious anxiety, expressed in the wish to restrict participants' possible encounters and prevent their free (mental) movement between the various parts of the system. Following the 'big
bang' which gave birth to the different groups, the following picture
emerged: of the fifty-two conference participants and six groups
formed, three were most conspicuous.[6] The biggest group consisted
of 20 participants who chose to adhere to the category of 'Other'.
Ironically enough, this group, too, quickly split into two: the group
of 'Other' and that of 'Other too'. This entire group, however, turned
out after closer scrutiny to in fact represent the parameter of Nationality (the 'real' Nationality group as opposed to the group that only
claimed to represent this parameter), as it was chiefly composed of
the American participants who had stated that they and their organizations were not represented in the conference's management.
Alongside this group, two other groups were formed which were
noticeably small. These were the Gender and the Race groups, equal
in size and gender distribution – two men and two women in each. It
was easy to see that this structure accurately reflected, along many
parameters, the structure of the management: two male directors
(Avi Nutkevitch and Mannie Sher) and two female administrators
(Dafna Bahat and Elaine Gallagher) or, alternatively, two male
directors and two female keynote speakers.

The central question examined in the group in which I participated was therefore the following: what is the significance of this
particular distribution of participants? How should we understand
the fact that of all the proposed parameters, it was those of gender
and race that generated an exact replica of the structure of the conference's management? How are we to understand the popularity of
'Other', and the fact that even the 'Other' group generated for itself
in the unconscious dynamic process a twin in its own image?

As we set out to find a hypothesis that could account for these
phenomena,[7] we noticed that Gender and Race are in fact the

[6] I shall only deal with these three here; other structures must have reflected other
aspects which will not be discussed in this paper.
[7] Many of the ideas brought here are the result of the collective group thinking that
took place in the Gender group as well as with other participants. Although none of
these other participants should be held accountable for what is written in this analysis, the credit for it should be shared with all of them, and particularly with my
colleague Allan Shaffer who greatly contributed to the ideas brought to these pages.

only parameters, among those proposed by the organizers, which cannot be chosen but are inherited by their owners. As such they are the most solid dimensions of identity, and their change (e.g., via genetic mutation) is catastrophic in terms of identity preservation. Did the fact that of all parameters, those two alone generated an exact replica of the structure of the conference's management, represent a wish that the knowledge that lies in the model should be transmitted (a little like nobility titles) and 'inherited', like some genetic information, from generation to generation, as is, without being exposed to far-reaching alterations, environmental influences of choice?

This assumption is to a certain degree confirmed by the story of the 'Other' group (which supposedly presents the reverse mirror image). The parameter of Nationality, in stark contrast with the parameters of Gender and Race, is a blunt and overt declaration of identity that can be adopted by choice. Moreover, unlike 'Other', which by definition emphasizes that which I am *not* (as it relies on that defining entity from which it differentiates itself by stating that it belongs to 'Other'), nationality defines what I *am*; not a negative but a positive definition. Why, then, did Nationality (in this case American) 'go underground' and hide itself under the guise of 'Other'? Moreover, and since we are in fact dealing with unconscious processes, why did 'Other' see fit to replicate itself in a mirror image ('Other Too'), if not to emphasize the system's (persistent) unconscious need to seek that which is similar and not that which is different, that which unites and not that which separates?

The homosexual dynamic has multiple facets and meanings; one of its most typical characteristics, however, is that it bears a possible solution to the oedipal rivalry that does not require 'patricide'; this is precisely one of the 'gains' of the homosexual solutions. In this solution the boys, the men, offer themselves in an act of submission and acceptance to the father, as they fantasize that a woman offers herself to a man. They thus – at least in Freud's view – avoid the risk of a confrontation with masculine authority, which in fantasy could have devastating results. Their identification with the woman (the mother) is supposed to take away the threat of rivalry with the father (and in this case with the knowledge he imparts). In the negative Oedipus, it is women who compete with the father, but as they are women they do not threaten his place in the same way masculine competition could.

The central working hypothesis I therefore wish to suggest is this: an exploration of the Tavistock model (using the Tavistock model's own tools) indicates that at the current stage of knowledge (the paradigm, in Kuhn's words), the scientific community identified with the model seeks to *confirm* the model, and not to challenge or refute it, or create a replacing or follow-up model, which could undermine the 'paternal authority' of those identified with it, namely, Miller and Rice. That could well be the outcome of the conference's closeness in time to Eric Miller's death. As if the unconscious question that had to be answered was 'who will inherit the knowledge?'. And that had to be found out without creating open rivalry between the 'successors', perhaps because we all shared the same anxiety and guilt feelings, namely, that our criticism is to be blamed for 'killing' our founding fathers.

Was the Belgirate Conference a sham exploration of the model? Has the anxiety created some sort of a defensive autistic self-exploration?

Far from it! Which brings me back to the Jewish tale I started with. Not only that an exploration based on yearning for confirmation through seeking the similar in the other is not autistic, but that it may, in spite of its defensive nature, open a vital inter-subjective process of validation and acknowledgement of the paradigm's self-worth. Neither the wish for confirmation nor the wish for innovation is in itself defensive or adaptive. As said before, the capacity for real development and creativity depends on the right mixture and balance of both forces in the learning process. Confirmation or ratification of that which already exists could turn out to be a necessary developmental stage in the life of *any* scientific model. Just as adolescents go through a 'homosexual phase' in their development (in the latency stage), which is essential to the stabilization of their gender identity before they mature to meet an other in the framework of a heterosexual interweave, so might the process of knowledge crystallization in the framework of a scientific paradigm require a similar phase of 'crystallization of identity' before it can open itself up to a productive exploration via that which is different or contradictory.

I believe that each new generation is bound to 'reinvent the wheel' in its own creative and unique way – in order 'to own' it. Despite the anxiety, which I think was a dominant factor in the learning process, the Belgirate Conference did make a significant contribution to the exploration of the model we currently hold.

But we should not ignore the danger that is now lurking on our doorstep; it is the danger – well known to anyone who ever tried to market a Tavistock conference – that the need to validate existing knowledge through that which is similar may lead to the creation of an 'aristocratic teaching' that only applies to those who have the same 'noble breeding', those whose heritage-inheritance makes them 'converted' in advance and who therefore 'fit' the model. The encounter with otherness still awaits us around the corner.

REFERENCES

Akoto, A. (1994) *Nationbuilding: Theory and Practice in Afrikan-centered Education*. Washington, DC: Pan Afrikan World Institute.

Armstrong, D. (1998) *The 'Institution in the Mind': Reflections on the Relation of Psycho-analysis to Work with Institutions*. London: Free Association Books.

Armstrong, D. (2002) The Work Group Revisited: reflections on the practice of group relations (lecture at the Tavistock Institute, February 2002).

Arnim, G. von (1997) Seinen ersten Deutschen traf er in Afrika: Der Botschafter Israels in Deutschland, Avi Primor, ist dort Anwalt Europas und muss hier oft 'Seelenklempner' sein. *Suedd. Zeitung*, Nr. 235, 13 Oktober: p. 10.

Azibo, D. A. (1989) African-centered theses on mental health and a nosology of Black/African personality disorder. *The Journal of Black Psychology*, 15(2): pp. 173–214.

Azibo, D. A. (1991) Diagnosing personality disorder in Africans (Blacks) using the Azibo nosology: Two case studies. *The Journal of Black Psychology*, 17(2): pp. 1–22.

Balint, M. (1968) *The Basic Fault*. London: Tavistock Publications.

Banet, A. G. & Hayden, C. (1977) The Tavistock primer. In: J. E. Jones, & J. W. Pfeiffer (Eds.). *The 1977 Handbook for Group Facilitators*. La Jolla, CA: University Associates, pp. 155–167.

Bateson, G. (1973) *Towards an Ecology of Mind*. St. Albans: Paladin.

Beland, H. (1990) Religiöse Wurzel des Antisemitismus. *Psyche, 45*: 458–470.

Benjamin, J. (1990) Recognition and destruction – An outline of intersubjectivity. In: A. S. Mitchell, & L. Aron (Eds.) *Relational Psychoanalysis: The Emergence of a Tradition*. London: The Analytic Press, pp. 181–210.

Bick, E. (1964) Notes on infant observations in psychoanalytic training. *International Journal of Psycho-analysis, 45*: pp. 558–566.

Biermann, C. (1995) Vorschlag zu einer künftigen Tagung der DPV: Trauer und Neubeginn in Deutschland nach dem Nazismus – Psychoanalyse transgenerationeller Beziehungen. *DPV-Informationen, 17* (May).

Bion, W. R. (1961) *Experiences in Groups and Other Papers*. London: Tavistock Publications.

Bion, W. R. (1962a) *Learning from Experience*. London. Karnac Books.

Bion, W. R. (1962b) The psycho-analytic study of thinking. *International Journal of Psycho-analysis, 43*: pp. 306–310.

Bion, W. R. (1963) *Elements of Psycho-Analysis*. London: Heinemann (reprinted London: Karnac Books, 1984).

Bion, W. R. (1970) *Attention and Interpretation*. London: Tavistock Publications.

Bion, W. R. (1973) Bion's Brazilian Lectures 1 and 2. Rio de Janeiro: Imago Editora. (Reprinted in one volume, London: Karnac Books, 1990.)

Bion, W. R. (1977) *Seven Servants. Four Works by Wilfred R. Bion*. New York: Jason Aronson.

Blumenberg, Y. (1995) *Book Review of Dührssen: Ein Jahrhundert Psychoanalytische Bewegung in Deutschland*. Tübingen: Luzifer-Amor 15.

Bollas, C. (1987) *The Shadow of the Object: Psychoanalysis of the Unthought Known*. London: Free Association Books.

Bott Spillius, E. (1992) Clinical experiences of projective identification. In: R. Anderson, (Ed.). *Clinical Lectures on Klein and Bion*. London and New York: Routledge.

Brecht, K. (1997) Die Teilung der psychoanalytischen Gemeinschaft in Deutschland und ihre Folgen. *DPV-Informationen, 21* (April).

Britton, R. (1992) 'The Oedipus situation and the depressive position', and 'Keeping things in mind'. In: R. Anderson (Ed.). *Clinical Lectures on Klein and Bion*. London and New York: Routledge.

Brown, R. (2000) *Group Processes*. Oxford: Blackwell Publishers.

Buber, M. (1960) (12. Auflage, 1996) *Der Weg des Menschen nach der chassidischen Lehre*. Gerlingen: Lambert Schneider.

Bynum, E. B. (1999) *The African Unconscious: Roots of Ancient Mysticism and Modern Psychology*. New York: Teachers College Press.

Bynum, E. B. (2000) *Research Methods in Clinical Psycho-Spirituality*. Amherst, MA: Obelisk Foundation, Inc.

Cooper, L., & Mack, C. (2003) Racism: Still alive and mostly unaccounted for. Paper presented at the Fourteenth Scientific Meeting, A. K. Rice Institute for the Study of Social Systems, MIT, Cambridge, MA.

Darling-Hammond, L. (1997) *The Right to Learn*. San Francisco, CA: Jossey-Bass Publishers.

Davis, M., & Wallbridge, D. (1981) *Boundary and Space: An Introduction to the Work of D. W. Winnicott*. London: Karnac Books.

Dewey, J. (1916) *Democracy and Education*. New York: The Free Press (reprinted 1944).

Dubois, W. E. B. (1973) Whither now and why? In: H. Aptheker (Ed.), *The Education of Black people: Ten Critiques, 1906–1960*. New York: Monthly Review Press.

Dührssen, A. (1994) *Ein Jahrhundert Psychoanalytische Bewegung in Deutschland: Die Psychotherapie unter dem Einfluss Freuds*. Göttingen: Vandenhoeck & Ruprecht.

Eliot, T. S. (1974) *Collected Poems 1909–1962*. London: Faber and Faber.

Erlich, H. S. (1992) On discourse with an enemy. In: E. R. Shapiro (Ed.), *The Inner World in the Outer World: Psychoanalytic Perspectives*. New Haven: Yale University Press, 1997, pp. 123–142.

Festinger, L. (1957) *A theory of cognitive dissonance*. Evanston, IL: Row, Peterson and Co.

Fine, M. (Ed.). (1994) *Chartering Urban School Reform: Reflections on Public High Schools in the Midst of Change*. New York: Teachers College Press.

Freud, S. (1911) *Formulations on the Two Principles of Mental Functioning*. Standard Edition, Vol. 12, London: Hogarth, pp. 215–226.

Gabelnick, F., & Carr, A. W. (Eds.) (1989) *Contributions to Social and Political Science. Proceedings of the First International Symposium on Group Relations, Keeble College, Oxford*. Washington, DC: A.K. Rice Institute.

Gertler, B., & Izod, K. (2004) Modernism and postmodernism in Group Relations: 'A Confusion of Tongues'. In: S. Cytrynbaum & D. A. Noumair (Eds.), *Group Relations Reader 3*. Jupiter, FL: The A. K. Rice Institute.

Gold, S., & Klein, L. (2004) Harold Bridger – Conversations and Recollections, *Organizational & Social Dynamics*, 4(1): 1–21.

Gosling, R. (1981) A study of very small groups. in Do I Dare Disturb the Universe? In: J. S. Grotstein (Ed.), *A Memorial to Wilfred Bion*. New York: Aaronson, pp. 634–645.

Gould, L. J. (1997) Correspondences between Bion's Basic Assumption Theory and Klein's Developmental Positions: An Outline. *Free Associations*, Vol. 7, Part 1(41): pp. 15–30.

Grinberg, L. (1979) Counter-transference and projective counter-identification. *Contemporary Psycho-Analysis*, 15: 226–247.

Grueneisen, V. (2003) Personal email communication, 25 October.

Grüner, S. (unpubl.) Bericht zur Arbeitstagung in Seeon (private correspondence).

Gutkowski, S., & Katz, E. (1988) Conflict and co-existence as manifested in consultation to a Jewish-Arab community. In: F. Gabelnick, & A. W. Carr (Eds.) (1989) Contributions to Social and Political Science. Proceedings of the First International Symposium on Group Relations, Keeble College, Oxford. Washington, DC: A. K. Rice Institute.

Hall, D. T., & Moss, J. E. (1998) The new protean career contract: Helping organisations and employees adapt. *Organisational Dynamics, 26(3)*: pp. 22–37. Quoted in: L. Holbeche (2000) *The Future of Careers*. Horsham: Roffey Park Institute Ltd.

Hatch, M. J. (1997) *Organisation Theory, Modern Symbolic and Postmodern Perspectives*. Oxford: Oxford University Press.

Hatch, T. (2001) It takes capacity to build capacity. *Education Week*, 14 February.

Hayden, C., & Molenkamp, R. J. (2002) *Tavistock Primer II*. Jupiter, FL: The A. K. Rice Institute for the Study of Social Systems.

Hillard, A. G. (1991) Do we have the will to educate all children? *Educational Leadership, 49*(1): 31–36.

Hillman, J. (1986) Notes on white supremacy: Essaying an archetypal account of historical events. *Spring publication: An Annual of Archetypal Psychology and Jungian Thought*: pp. 29–58.

Hinschelwood, R. D., & Skogstad, W. (2000) *Observing Organisations: Anxiety, Defence and Culture in Health Care*. London and Philadelphia: Routledge.

Hirschhorn, L. (1988) *The Workplace Within: Psychodynamics of Organisational Life*. Cambridge, MA: MIT Press.

Holbeche, L. (2000) *The Future of Careers*. Horsham: Roffey Park Institute Ltd.

Holvino, E. (2003) The Application of the Third Way: The Integration of the NTL and Tavistock Group Work in Organisational Consultation. Presented at the Fourteenth Scientific Meeting, A. K. Rice Institute for the Study of Social System. MIT, Cambridge, MA.

Hupkens, L. A. J. (1995a) Unconscious processes in organisations: my experience with Group Relations conferences. Newsletter of the NVOA Netherlands Network of Women Management Consultants, December.

Hupkens, L. A. J. (1995b) Working with un/subconscious processes in organisations, *Journal of the Netherlands Council for Management Consultants, 5*.

Hupkens, L. A. J. (1999) What do you mean, unconscious processes in organisations? *Groeps Psycho Therapie*, December: pp. 223–229.

Hutton, J., Bazalgette, J., & Reed, B. (1997) Organisation-in-the-mind. In: J. Neumann, K. Kellner, A. Dawson-Shepherd (Eds.) *Developing Consultancy*. London: Routledge.

Jaques, E. (1955) Social systems as a defence against persecutory and depressive anxiety. In: M. Klein, P. Heimann, & R. E. Money-Kyrle (Eds.), *New Directions in Psychoanalysis*. London: Tavistock Publications.

Jaques, E. (1976) *A General Theory of Bureaucracy*. London: Heinemann, pp. 106–108.

Jaques, E. (1989) *Requisite Organisation*. Arlington, VA: Cason Hall & Co.

Klein, E. B., Gabelnick, F., & Herr, P. (1998) *The Psychodynamics of Leadership*. Madison, CN: Psychosocial Press.

Klein, M. (1930) The importance of symbol-formation in the development of the ego. In: *Contributions to Psycho-analysis*. New York: McGraw Hill, 1964.

Klein, M. (1935) A contribution to the psychogenesis of manic depressive states. In: M. Klein (1975) *Vol. I*.

Klein, M. (1940) Mourning and its relation to manic-depressive states. In: *Love, Guilt and Reparation*. London: Virago, 1988.

Klein, M. (1946a) Notes on some schizoid mechanisms. In: *Envy and Gratitude*. London: Virago, 1988.

Klein, M. (1946b) Notes on some schizoid mechanisms. In: M. Klein (1975) *Vol. III*.

Klein, M. (1975) *The Writings of Melanie Klein. Vols. I & III*, London: Hogarth.

Krantz, J. and Gilmore, T. (1990) Projective Identification in Organisational Consultation from www.triadllc.com/pubprojective.html

Kremer, R. (1997) Bericht über die Arbeitskonferenz 'Die Teilung der psychoanalytischen Gemeinschaft in Deutschland und ihre Folgen' vom 3. bis 7.7.96 im Kloster Seeon. *DPV-Informationen 21* (April).

Kreuzer-Haustein, U. (1996) Die Teilung der psychoanalytischen Gemeinschaft in Deutschland und ihre Folgen. *Forum der Psychoanalyse*, Band 12: Heft 4, Dezember.

Krieger, L. H. (1995) The content of our categories: A cognitive bias approach to discrimination and equal employment opportunity. *Stanford Law Review*, 47: 1161–1248.

Kristol, I. (1997) Conflicts that can't be resolved. *The Wall Street Journal Europe*, XV: p. 152, September 8.

Kuhn, T. (1962) *The Structure of Scientific Revolution*. Chicago, IL: University of Chicago Press.

Lawrence. W. G. (1979) *Exploring Individual and Organisational Boundaries: A Tavistock Open Systems Approach*. New York: John Wiley & Sons.

Lawrence, W. G., Bain, A., & Gould, L. (1996) The fifth basic assumption. *Free Associations*, 6(Part 1, no. 37): 28–35.

Mack, C. (1979) Old assumptions and new packages: Racism, educational models and Black children. *Young Children, XIX(6)*: 45–51.

Mack, C. (1981) Emotional disturbance and Afro-American children and youth: An ecological view, in B. A. Coppock, Jr., & F. H. Wood (Eds), *Issues in Education and Mental Health of Afro-American Children and Youth with Behavior and Emotional Problems.* St. Paul, MN: University of Minnesota Press.

Mack, C. (1993) Awakening the Afro-centric: Roots and Developmental States. Paper presented at the African American Leadership Conference, Southern University, Baton Rouge, LA.

Meier, D. (1995) *The Power of their Ideas: Lessons for America from a Small School in Harlem.* Boston: Beacon Press.

Menzies Lyth, I. (1988) *Containing Anxiety in Institutions: Selected Essays. Vol. 1.* London: Free Association Books.

Miller, E. J. (1977) Organisational development and industrial democracy: a current case-study. In: C. Cooper (Ed.) *Organisational Development in the UK and USA: A Joint Evaluation.* New York: Macmillan, 31–63.

Miller, E. J. (1983) Work and Creativity, Occasional Paper No. 6, Tavistock Institute of Human Relations.

Miller, E. J. (1989) The Leicester Model, Experiential Study of Group and Organisational Processes, Occasional Paper, No. 10, Tavistock Institute of Human Relations.

Miller, E. J. (1993a) (unpublished) The Vicissitudes of Identity. Opening Address to the International Group Relations and Scientific Conference: Exploring Global Social Dynamics, Lorne, Victoria.

Miller, E. J. (1993b) *From Dependency to Autonomy.* Free Association Books, London.

Miller, E. J., & Rice, A. K. (1967) *Systems of Organisation.* London: Tavistock Publications.

Miller, J. C. (1977) The Psychology of Conflict in Belfast: Conference as Microcosm. *Journal of Personality and Social Systems, 1*(1) (April).

Morgan, G. (1986) *Images of Organisation.* London: Sage Publications.

Murphy, D. (2002) District thoughts regarding closing the educational achievement gap and creating a positive school climate. Davis, CA: Davis Unified School District.

Nahum, T., & Shafer, A. T. (2000) The role of the 'Conference Administrator'. Paper presented at the 2nd Scientific Conference of the Australian Institute of Socio-Analysis. Canberra.

Nedelman, C. (1997) Nachbemerkungen zur ersten DPG-DPV Konferenz. *DPV-Informationen, 22* (October).

Neumann, J., & Hirschhorn, L. (1999) The Challenge of Integrating Psychodynamic and Organisational Theory. *Human Relations, 52*: 683–695.

Obholzer, A., & Roberts, V. Z. (Eds.) (1994) *The Unconscious at Work.* London: Routledge.

Ogden, T. H. (1994) *Subjects of Analysis.* Northvale, NJ: Jason Aronson.

Palmer, B (1979) Learning and the group experience. In: W. G. Lawrence

(Ed.), *Exploring Individual and Organisational Boundaries*. London: Wiley, pp. 169–192.

Phillips, C. B. (1998) *Culture: A Process that Empowers*. Washington, DC: Black Child Development Institute.

Pine, F. (1988) The Four Psychologies of Psychoanalysis and their Place in Clinical Work. *Journal American Psychoanalytical Associationn, 36*: 571–596.

Powell, L., & Barber, M. (2004) Savage inequities indeed: Unconscious processes in educational transformation. In: S. Cytrynbaum, & D. A. Noumair (Eds.), *Group Relations Reader 3*. Jupiter, FL: The A. K. Rice Institute.

Reed, B. (1988) An Exploration of Role as Used in the Grubb Institute. Unpublished paper.

Reed, B. D. (1976) Organisational Role Analysis. In: C. L. Cooper (Ed.) *Developing Social Skills in Managers: Advances in Group Training*. London: Macmillan.

Rice, A. K. (1965) *Learning for Leadership*. London: Tavistock Publications.

Richards, D. M. (1980) *Let the Circle be Unbroken: The Implications of African Spirituality in the Diaspora*. Trenton, NJ: The Red Sea Press.

Richardson, E. (1967) *The Environment of Learning*. London: Thomas Nelson and Sons Ltd.

Rioch, M. J. (1971) 'Are we like sheep' (Isaiah 53:6): Followers and leaders. *Psychiatry, 34*: pp. 258–273. Also in A. D. Colman, & W. H. Bexton (Eds), *Group Relations Reader I*. Washington, DC: A. K. Rice Institute.

Rothenburg, C. (1997) Die Teilung der psychoanalytischen Gemeinschaft in Deutschland und ihre Folgen: Ein persönlicher Bericht über die Teilnahme an der Arbeitskonferenz vom 3. bis 7. Juli 1996 in Seeon. *DPV-Informationen*, 21 (April).

Schein, E. H. (1992) *Organisational Culture and Leadership*. San Francisco, CA: Jossey-Bass Publishers.

Schuetz, A. (1944) The stranger: An essay in social psychology. *The American Journal of Sociology, 49*(6): 499–507.

Segal, H. (1973) *Introduction to the Work of Melanie Klein*. London: Hogarth.

Shafer, A. (2003) Developing the 'Socio-Analytic Mind' in Australia: A Socio-Analytic Exploration of the Key Themes of Major Group Relations Programmes of the Australian Institute of Socio-Analysis: 1987–2003. *Organisational & Social Dynamics, 3*(2): 267–276.

Shafer, A. (2003) Mental Health Organisations and the Problem of 'Management'. Paper presented at the OPUS Conference 'Organisational and Social Dynamics: International Perspectives from Group Relations, Psychoanalysis and Systems Theory', London.

Shapiro, D. (1965) *Neurotic Styles*. New York: Basic Books. Quoted in A. Mitchell Steven (1988) *Relational Concepts in Psychoanalysis*. Cambridge, MA: Harvard University Press, p. 254.

Shujaa, M. J. (1994) Education and Schooling: You Can have One Without the Other. In: Mwalimu J. Shujaa (Ed), *Too Much Schooling, Too Little Education: A Paradox of Black Life in White Societies*. Trenton, N.J.: African World Press, Inc., pp. 13–36.

Smircich, L. (1983) Concepts of Culture and Organisational Analysis. *Administrative Science Quarterly*, 28: pp. 339–358.

Stacey, R. (2001) Complexity at the 'Edge' of the Basic-Assumption Group. In: L. Gould, L. Stapley, & M. Stein (Eds.). *The Systems Psychodynamics of Organisations*. London: Karnac Books.

Stein, M. (1995) Organisational life as spiritual practice. In: M. Stein, & J. Hollwitz (Eds.), *Psyche at Work: Workplace Applications of Jungian Analytical Psychology*. Wilmette, IL: Chiron Publications, pp. 1–18.

Steiner, J. (1993) *Psychic Retreats*. London: Routledge.

Symington, J., & Symington, N. (1996) *The Clinical Thinking of Wilfred Bion*. London: Routledge.

Trimborn, W. (1997) Report of the DPG-DPV Conference in Frankfurt. *DPV-Informationen*, 22 (October).

Trist, E. L., & Sofer, C. (1959) *Exploration in Group Relations*. (Leicester University Press).

Tyack, D. B., & Cuban, L. (1995) *Tinkering Toward Utopia: A Century of Public School Reform*. Cambridge, MA: Harvard University Press.

Westlander, G. (2000) Forskarroller i varianter av aktionsforskning. [Researcher roles in action research] *Nordisk Psykologi, 52*(3): 197–216.

Wheatley, M. J. (1992) *Leadership and the New Science: Learning about Organisation from an Orderly Universe*. San Francisco, CA: Berrett-Koehler Publishers, Inc.

Williams, R. (1974) *Cognitive and Survival Learning of the Black Child. The Survival of Black Children and Youth*. Washington, DC: Nuclassics and Science Publishing Co.

Winnicott, D. W. (1960) Ego distortions in terms of true and false self. In: *The Maturational Processes and the Facilitating Environment*. London: Karnac Books, pp. 140–152.

Winnicott, D. W. (1971) *Playing and Reality*. London: Tavistock Publications.

Woodson, C. (1933) *Miseducation of the Negro*. Washington, DC: Associated Publishers (reprinted 1969).

Zitzelberger-Schlez, A. (1994) Bericht von der Arbeitskonferenz 'Germans and Israelis: The Past in the Present'. *DPV-Informationen, 16* (November).

INDEX

Abraham, Karl, 63
achievement gap, 77–78, 94–107
action learning set, 87–89, 91
action research, 77, 106, 119
administrator, conference, 6,
        132–133
affect, 100
African-American students *see* black
        students
AKRI, 11
anti-psychoanalytic ideas and
        beliefs, 72
anxiety, 15, 18
    Belgirate Conference, 174–178
    defence against by university
        clinic, 115–116
    and experiential learning, 18, 20,
        23–25
    of failure, 109
    public school organisations, 100,
        102–103
    structure and design of
        conferences, 36–37
    toleration of and learning,
        170–173
anxious edge, 20–21, 162

application of learning, 121–122,
        123–137
    by conference members, 121–122,
        124–128
    in daily work of consultants and
        managers, 121–122, 138–150
    to institutions and organisations,
        25–29, 80–84
    by staff and sponsoring
        institutions, 121–122, 128–37
application groups, 26–27, 34,
        126–127, 154–155
    see also review and application
        groups (RAGs)
aristocratic teaching, 180
Armstrong, D., 32, 157
assumptions, basic, 78, 108–120
Australian Institute of
        Socio-Analysis (AISA),
        123–137
    demise of, 136
    half-day event for conference
        participants, 128–130
    learning from conferences,
        129–130, 132–135, 136–137
    2003 Conference, 128